52 THINGS

TO SEE AND DO
in Basilicata

52 THINGS
TO SEE AND DO
in Basilicata

BY VALERIE FORTNEY

Copyright © 2020 by Valerie Fortney
All Rights Reserved

Published by My Bella Vacanza Press

Cover Photos: Peperoni cruschi; port of Maratea; city of Matera.
All cover photos are my own, copyrights reserved.

Book design by Maureen Cutajar

For Mama Jo

Tu sei la mia stella brillante per sempre

CONTENTS

Preface viii
Benvenuti in Basilicata!. 1
Practical Information. 8
Planning Your Trip to Basilicata. 10
A Brief Basilicata History Timeline 15
Basilicata by the Numbers 22

MATERA PROVINCE

Matera: The Jewel of Basilicata 25
1. Swim In A Cave (And Sleep In One, Too!) 30
2. Hear The Sound Of Music In Matera 33
3. Matera Reflect At The Sistine Chapel Of The South . . 36
4. Get Into Some Metal Rock In Matera 39
5. Do Some Carbo-Loading In Matera 43
6. Drink With The Stars In Bernalda 46
7. Get Philosophical In Metaponto 49
8. Go To "That Town" That Nobody Names 52
9. Meet The Sea Turtles In Policoro. 55
10. Search For Ghosts In A Real, Live (Um) Ghost Town 58
11. Follow The Footsteps of an Exiled Rebel in Aliano . . 61
12. Drink To Your Digestion. 65
13. Look for Invaders from the Tower in Tricarico 68

14. Find the Lost Utopia at Campomaggiore Vecchio ... 71
15. Go Coast To Coast. 75

POTENZA PROVINCE

Maratea: The Pearl of Basilicata 79
16. Make A Splash In Maratea 83
17. Walk In The Footsteps Of A Saint 88
18. Marvel at the Grotta delle Meraviglie 91
19. Row, Row, Row Your Boat (Or Cheat With A Motor) . 94
20. Explore Your Wild Side in the Pollino National Park . 97
21. Indulge in Modern Art in the Pollino National Park 100
22. Attend A Weird Wedding. 103
23. Bite into the S-Crunch-Ous Peperoni 106
24. Revel in the Little Pompeii of Basilicata. 109
25. Pay Homage to the Queen of Basilicata in Viggiano . 112
26. Strum a Song on a Harp in Viggiano 116
27. Eat to Your Heart in Sarconi 119
28. Go to the Moon (and back) in Sasso di Castalda. . . 122
29. Take a Walk with the Forest in Satriano di Lucania . 125

POTENZA

The Capital City 129
30. Ride Europe's Longest Escalator in Potenza. 132
31. Go Hog Wild and Eat a Piece of History 135
32. At Muro Lucano, Cross that Bridge 138
33. Give Your True Love...A Dagger? 141
34. Bring On The Baccalà. 144
35. Join A Band Of Brigands 147
36. Star Gazing and Arabian Nights in Pietrapertosa . . 150
37. Fly with the Angels at Castelmezzano 153

38. Get Fired Up at Italy's Largest Bonfire 157
39. Gaze at the Heavens – and Some Heavenly Art 160
40. Taste One of Italy's Most Prized Cheeses in Abriola . 163
41. Time Travel with the Holy Roman Emperor 166
42. Visit Albania in the Heart of Basilicata 169
43. Surround Yourself with Saints in Ripacandida 173
44. Cool Down in the Cascades at San Fele 176
45. Seize The Day In Venosa 179
46. Cross the Abbey Road in Venosa 182
47. Enjoy a Pedal-Powered Day at a Volcanic Lake 185
48. Follow the Footsteps of History in Melfi 188
49. Storm the Castle in Melfi 191
50. Sip One of Italy's Oldest Wines 194
51. Search for the Holy Grail in Acerenza 198
52. Travel the World in One Region – or Pretend To . . . 203

Basilicata's Foodie Delights 206
Ten Stand-Out Restaurants 211
Hotels In Basilicata 216
Resources 221
Afterword 224
Grazie… 225
Photo Credits 224
About the Author 225

Preface

My husband Bryan and I first came to Basilicata in 2003 to see the towns where my grandmother's family came from, accompanied by my mom and my sister. That first visit made quite an impression. We stood in wonder on the top of Monte Siri with the town of Anzi staggering down the steep hill below us, and unbroken natural beauty unfolding for miles in our sweeping view. It seemed incredible that my ancestors would leave such a gorgeous land for flat and unremarkable small-town Ohio. Of course, the beauty meant nothing if they couldn't eke out an income or enough to subsist on, and they emigrated like so many others during the first decade of the 20th century.

We returned a few years later with my cousins, and that trip led to a heart-warming discovery -we had relatives living in Anzi; they didn't just acknowledge us, they embraced us, and took us into the fold of the *famiglia*. After moving to Italy, Bryan and I traveled from Ascoli Piceno (Marche) to Basilicata on many occasions, for town *festas*, family feasts, and general exploration. We fell in love with the people and the landscapes, the long-standing traditions, the uniqueness and sense of place. We bought our *piccola casa* in 2010 and have been here ever since.

Our explorations have continued as we seek out the intriguing places, little-known sights, and interesting quirks this region holds. Our friends tell us "*conoscete meglio voi la Basilicata che noi!*" (You know Basilicata better than we do!) Like often happens, those who live in a place can take it for granted and not visit the sights that are right in their backyard. We've made an effort to know this place that goes by two names-Lucania and Basilicata- to see it, to really experience it. As we've immersed ourselves, we've become a part of our community, and have been made to feel like locals through the extraordinary hospitality the residents offer. I knew we'd really been accepted when a local author wrote a dedication in my copy of her book: To my American friend with a Lucanian soul.

Come and discover the heart and soul of this place that I call home. You'll see why it drew me, and why it remains an almost-mystical land that is part of Italy and yet set apart in its own storied traditions and raw beauty. I know you'll leave with a lot of photos and cherished memories at discovering such an interesting, little-known place.

– Valerie

Benvenuti In Basilicata!

Welcome to Basilicata, a region of wonders and natural splendor. Steeped in history, you'll find this small southern region has it all – hilltop hamlets, captivating castles, breathtaking scenery, and fascinating sights and festivals. Top it off with warm welcomes and fabulous food (and wine!), and you will be glad you came.

Basilicata is one of the least-known and least-populated regions in Italy. It is cuddled between Puglia, Campania, and Calabria, forming the boot's oft-overlooked ankle and part of the instep. While Basilicata can boast two slices of coast on two different seas, its bulk is made up of mountains and hills. There are billowing wheat fields, olive groves and vine-striped hills. But there are also rocky and rugged mountains where squiggly roads reach towns that seem stopped in time, clinging to ridges and slopes. The landscapes here have a raw and awesome beauty, and it changes every few miles. Francis Ford Coppola, whose roots are here, said, "When you see Basilicata you see fields, vineyards, beautiful landscapes. You see the land as it should be." I say Amen to that.

The region's history is truly ancient – before Rome was founded and before Solomon's temple was built, this region was already ancient. I have included a timeline for easy reference, but there are a few details to know. The area was called Lucania, so-named for the Lucani people, an Italic tribe that spoke Oscan and held ties with the Samnites (who populated Abruzzo, Molise and part of Campania). Lucania was part of what the colonizing Greeks called Enotria (which means "land of vineyards" and where the word "oenophile" originates). The name Lucania may derive from *lucus*, meaning sacred wood; some believe it more probably came from *leukos*, meaning shining, luminous. Still others say the name is from the Greek *lykos*, or wolf. The Lucani expanded their territory to the west, encompassing the Mediterranean coast (now the Cilento, south of Salerno), conquering the Greek city of Poseidonia, which the Lucani called Paistom (and the Romans called Paestum), extending the Grande Lucania down the coast. The Magna Grecia colony they overran referred to them as the *terribili Lucani*. Indeed, they became known as fierce warriors.

Basilicata came into play in the 11th or 12th century and again there is some debate about the name's origins. It may have been designated by the Byzantines; the title given to governors was Basilikos. Or, some hold it comes from Basilica, specifically the one in Acerenza (#51), the archbishop having been given jurisdiction over a vast territory. The name was changed back to Lucania for a brief spell, from 1932-1947, but reverted again to Basilicata with the formation of the Republic of Italy. (Is it any wonder the region has a bit of an identity crisis?)

Today both names are used rather interchangeably, but whatever you call the region, don't call the inhabitants a Basilicatan or *Basilicatesi*. They are proudly known as Lucani still today.

The Fall of Rome and the Middle Ages brought a string of foreign rulers, starting with the Byzantines, then the Lombards, the Normans and Swabians; from 1302 the entire south of Italy was under the Kingdom of Naples. When Garibaldi swept through and presented the south to the Savoy rulers, a popular uprising took place here in an effort to have a say in their own destiny. Known as *briganti* (#35) they battled the trained military forces for nearly ten years before being subdued. The absorption into the Kingdom of Italy brought punitive measures and economic hardship that led millions to leave southern Italy in search of improved conditions and jobs abroad.

Basilicata remained a forgotten and overlooked land for decades, but the good Lucani carried on their traditions all the same. I like to say that Italians dwell in their history, and here especially, the millennia of experience still resonate; old ways are still maintained, kept alive by centuries of relative isolation and the tenacious pride of the Lucani people. Today, visitors most often leave Basilicata with a lasting impression, using the words "untouched" and "authentic" to describe it.

The cultural blending of Greek (#7), Norman, Byzantine, Albanian (#42) and Arab (#36) create an almost exotic aura, with events that date back centuries (or more) that blend sacred and pagan rituals together. The region's natural beauty is pristine and primeval, with breathtaking panoramas that take in snow-frosted peaks and mountain splendor in its two national parks – the Pollino National Park (#20), and Parco Nazionale dell'Appennino Lucano- along with a few large forested regional parks. In fact, 47% of the land is mountainous, and another 45% covered in hills, leaving a mere 8% of flat plains, around Metaponto. The two pieces of coastline are small, but pack a punch; the unbroken stretch of sand on the Ionian Sea (#9) contrasts distinctly from the rollicking rocky coast at Maratea (#16). For visitors, that all adds up to an abundance of outdoors activities, along with folk festivals (#22 and #29), ancient ruins (#24), and historic castles (#41 and #49). You'll find glorious cathedrals along with more humble churches adorned with breathtaking art.

The Lucani are down-to-earth, no-nonsense folks; while you may feel they're staring at you, they are quick to return a smile. They give the same look to everyone who comes from outside the town, even Romans or Pugliesi. They are hospitable to the max, and are likely to take you by the hand to help show you the way, and offer you a coffee in the meantime. They have a saying here: *L'ospitalità è sacra*, hospitality is sacred. And they take it seriously.

Then there's the food. *Mangiamo*! The genuine homegrown and home-cooked specialties alone make it worth the trip. The region makes use of that level coastal plain to grow loads of produce like eggplant, artichokes, zucchini, and tomatoes, along with citrus, peaches and apples, and strawberries. (Oh, the strawberries.) Most folks keep an *orto* (vegetable patch) even in the mountains. Wheat fields are found even on steep hills, but especially the low rippling ones near Melfi, milled in the region for the flour that goes into the excellent bread (#5), pasta and more. Everything is enjoyed in its season, at its freshest, and the flavors will astound you. One friend commented, "It's like I've never tasted a real tomato before now!"

The pasta shapes that are most used here are *cavatelli*, *strascinati* and *orecchiette*, and they match well with beans (#27), chickpeas, and vegetables like rapini (called *cima di ràpe* here); another legume they love is the heritage *cicerchia*, which is sort of like a cross between a chickpea and a fava bean. The defining food is a dried sweet pepper, called *peperoni cruschi* (#23), which you simply must taste. They love their forest-foraged *cardoncelli* mushrooms here, and you will too; black truffles are a mountain treat, as well.

Many peasant dishes are exulted for their simplicity and ingenuity, like *acqua sale* (which literally means salt water), an ingenious way to use stale bread. *Pane cotto* (cooked bread) takes various vegetables cooked in broth and pours it over dry bread. For meat, the reigning king is Pig, which many families still raise to make the various salamis like *soppressata* and *capocollo*, either *dolce* (sweet) or *piccante* (spicy); and the fresh sausages *lucanica* (#31) and *pezzente*. Don't overlook lamb, though, as they are raised here and dishes using it are absolutely delicious. Try the lamb and potatoes roasted in the oven, or a lamb stew called *cutturidd'*. They love to grill it, too. (See my food run-down at the back.)

The wine. Oh yes, this part will make you swoon (the ancient Romans sure did!). Aglianico del Vulture (#50) is an underrated heavy-hitter that is starting to gain more international attention, so be sure to taste it; you'll find it pairs perfectly with the region's dishes.

Yes, Basilicata has it all, except tons of tourists. Even Matera and Maratea for all their glories and attention aren't jam-packed. That means you get the sense of discovery, of uncrowded enjoyment. The other thing the region lacks? Information in English. That's why I've written this book. My aim is to provide you with a useful resource to help you make the most of your trip. It's certainly not complete; and it was definitely hard narrowing it down. I've selected things to appeal to every taste, so while one activity might not be your thing, there are certainly others that will be. And (and!) you'll quickly see that there are **many, many more** than 52 things included, as almost every entry also refers to several other sights and places. I've also included a run-down on the foods, and a bonus, Ten Restaurants That Are Worth the Trip; you'll eat well everywhere, but these are my personal picks for standout dining experiences. I also know from experience that suitable lodgings can be hard to find; many places have a paltry online presence, so I've listed some hotels to help you along. There are certainly many others, and you'll find those through the booking sites and online searches. And I give you an informative listing of the signature foods, too.

With just 600,000 residents, the region is divided into only two provinces: **Potenza**, the regional capital as well as provincial capital; and **Matera**. I've started with Matera, the most renowned city and followed a rough geographical plan through that province, moving over to the southern end of the Potenza province and then tracking northward in a wide loop.

Now you're ready; let's pack up and travel around my *bella Basilicata*!

Practical Information

Getting Here and Getting Around

Tucked away in southern Italy's "ankle" between Salerno and Bari (Campania and Puglia), Basilicata sits in a mid-way position. The ancient Roman roads Via Appia and Via Herculia passed through, and the region was once a crossroads of cultures.

Nowadays, it's somewhat better connected but there is no airport in the region, and reaching many of the smaller towns can be difficult by public transit. Having a car is the easiest way to explore Basilicata, especially if you're venturing beyond Matera. If you absolutely don't want to drive, I have some alternate options for you below.

ARRIVING BY TRAIN: Trenitalia has service to Potenza, with stops along the Basento valley, continuing on to Metaponto. The rail stations for those towns are a distance from the town centers, though, so it is difficult to get from the station to the village. High speed options on **Trenitalia**'s Freccia Rossa and the private **Italo Treno** get you to Potenza and Matera with their own connecting bus service (one ticket for the full service). For example, from Rome to Matera you book a ticket through to Matera; take the Italo Treno high speed service to Salerno with a connection by ItaloBus to Matera. The bus will be outside the Salerno station to take you the rest of the journey. (It's the same drill for Trenitalia's connecting service.)

TO POTENZA AND BEYOND. You can take the train to Potenza then get a local bus to the town of your choice (depending on the town). You would need to look up the *autolinea* that serves the town. Example: From Potenza to Trivigno, the bus company Autolinea Genovese runs several times a day. To Albano di Lucania it is Autolinea Savitour. Frequency varies by town and bus company.

MATERA. You can arrive in Matera from Bari with Ferrovia Appulo Lucano train. There are also many driver services between Bari and Matera, by far the easiest option.

FROM ROME TO POTENZA OR MATERA BY MOTOR COACH – the companies Liscio, Marozzi and FlixBus all provide service. See the Resources section in the back for links.

You will find more information on connections to Matera at www.materaturismo.it/en/how-to-get-to-matera.

A private driver may be your best option for exploring without a rental car. They can schedule for your desires, so you avoid having to spend precious vacation time waiting for buses or trains. You also don't want to cut your time short because you have to rush back to the bus. See Resources for a short list.

Driving in Basilicata isn't especially difficult. The region is sparsely inhabited so you don't have lots of chaotic traffic to contend with. Honestly, a rental car gives you the best flexibility and mobility for getting to and around the region.

Planning Your Trip to Basilicata

As glorious as the scenery is, and as welcoming as the Lucani are, you would think they would extend that energy to their online presence. Alas. Not so much. While I've seen an impressive gain in that department, many businesses still do not have a web presence, or they throw up a site and never touch it again.

The good news is many more accommodations providers have joined in with online booking, either on their own or through a reservations conglomerate like Booking.com and the like. If the inn or apartment stay that you are interested in has a website, do send them an email about reservations. Just give them a little bit of time; most don't respond within 24 hours but rather within a few days. I highly recommend reserving in advance; just showing up and trying to find lodgings may be problematic, not to mention time consuming and frustrating.

See my list of faves at the back of the book. I've chosen a selection based mostly on ambiance, friendliness and overall experience, with an eye on price, too.

For the museums, archeological sites, and attractions, be sure to check their opening days and hours before heading out. As I mentioned, the websites may not have been updated recently, so a phone call will be your best bet.

Weather and Packing

Basilicata may be small but the climate zones change fairly drastically around the region, so the average in Metaponto is totally different than the weather you'll find in Pietrapertosa. The mountains certainly keep things cooler, and even in August, the evenings at higher altitudes will be chilly once the sun goes down. I have been at *festas* on summer nights where I needed not just a jacket but a sweater, too! Generally, the areas closer to the seas are more humid, while the upper elevations tend to be drier.

Winters are of course milder at lower elevations, and can be downright frigid in the mountains, especially when it snows. But there is also a special beauty here when everything is powdered white.

General Tips

The south of Italy in general, and Basilicata in particular, still observe the rhythm of the day that has marked life here for generations. In practical terms, that means that everything closes down between 1:00 or 1:30 PM for a long lunch and *riposo* (siesta). It's the ideal time to get out and photograph the empty streets, take a country walk with no traffic, or do like the Lucani and take a post-*pranzo* nap. Things reopen between 4:00 to 5:00 PM.

Lunch is usually from 1:00 – 2:30 PM if you're dining out; a few places may open earlier, around 12:30, especially if they tend to cater to workers. There are many places where "*si mangia bene e si paga poco*" (you eat well, and pay little). Dinner is generally between 8:00 -9:30 PM; while most of our friends prefer to eat between 8:00-8:30 pm, others are just getting home from work so dinner gets pushed back. In the summer, it tends to be later as they wait for the heat to subside.

One more note: lunch is still the larger meal of the day for most folks here. The family gathers together, and rather than a quick sandwich, they'll have a nice plate of pasta with some vegetables and salad, maybe a meat dish, too. Dinner is usually lighter unless they're dining out with friends; then it's an occasion and it will be a bigger meal.

That doesn't mean the Lucani don't enjoy a picnic. There are plenty of shops to get the fixings or order sandwiches and other goodies to take along for a lunch in the countryside or on the beach.

Watch and Read

There aren't loads of books about the region, but a few are worthwhile reads before your trip.

Christ Stopped at Eboli by Carlo Levi. The famous book by a political dissident exiled in Aliano, recounting the people and way of life he encountered there during the dark, economically depressed days between the two world wars.

Under the Southern Sun by Paul Paolicelli. A well-researched look at southern Italy, the misunderstood history, and the characteristics of southern Italians that helped them succeed in America.

Seasons in Basilicata by David Yeadon. An English writer spends a year in Aliano revisiting Carlo Levi's famous book, and how things have changed (and not) through the years.

Been Here a Thousand Years by Mariolina Venezia. A multigenerational saga following the Falcone family's joys and tears, taking in more than a century of southern Italy history along the way. Set in Grottole.

Finding Marco by Kenneth Cancellara. An Italian-American CEO returns to his birthplace of Acerenza to rediscover himself as he struggles with the desire for a simpler life versus the power, rewards and stress of corporate life.

FILMS: There have been a good number of movies filmed here, especially in recent years. A few to check out:

Basilicata Coast to Coast. A quirky hit movie that follows a band as they walk from Maratea to Scanzano Jonico as a publicity stunt. The scenery highlights beautiful places along the way.

Un Paese Quasi Perfetto. Filmed in Castelmezzano and Pietrapertosa, the cute comedy of a declining village brings a northern doctor to town, with funny and touching scenes.

No Time to Die and *Quantum of Solace.* Both of these James Bond movies came to Matera for filming, but No Time to Die especially shows the city to great effect.

Ben Hur. The remake with Morgan Freeman may not have gone down well with fans, but many key scenes were shot in Matera.

The Passion of the Christ. Filmed in Matera and Craco, the streets of the Sassi were perfect stand-ins for Jerusalem.

Christ Stopped at Eboli. The film adaptation of Carlo Levi's book, scenes were filmed in Aliano, Craco, Guardia Perticara and Matera.

A Brief Basilicata History Timeline

Prehistoric 3000-1000 BC

In the Paleolithic era hunters and gathers occupied parts of the region, living near rivers and lakes in huts or caves. Extinct animal fossils have been found, and cave petroglyphs and paintings testify of their existence. The Iron Age brought an increase in political and commercial contact with the Etruscans, Phoenicians and native tribes of surrounding areas.

The Lucani and the Greeks 700-300 BC

The Lucani occupied the inner territory of the region, and then extended their realm to the Mediterranean coast, what is now the Cilento Coast, creating a large area known as *la Grande Lucania*.

The warrior-like people were called *i terribili Lucani* by the Greeks at Paestum and Velia who were overtaken by them. The Lucani may have been descended from the Samnites who occupied parts of Campania, Molise and Abruzzo. They didn't leave behind large towns or a wealth of artifacts like the Etruscans, but sites like Serra del Vaglio and the Santuario di Rossano, also near Vaglio, testify to their presence and religious practices. Coins, jewelry and other items are in the Archeology Museum in Potenza (#30). A side note: the acclaimed tomb paintings found at the Greek temples of Paestum were painted by Lucanian artists.

The Greeks arrived and established colonies around southern Italy, including in Lucania, at Metaponto, Eraklea (modern Policoro), Siris (Nova Siri) and Taras (now Tursi). Along with colonies in Calabria and Campania, the area was called Magna Grecia (Greater Greece). Pythagoras arrived in Metaponto around 510 BC, continuing his school of philosophy, metaphysics and mathematics until his death around 495 BC.

THE ROMANS

400 BC – 400 AD: The Via Appia reached from Rome to Brindisi (Puglia) by way of Lucania, with branching roads, Via Herculia and Via Popilia that crossed Lucania. The Romans subdued the Lucani and established flourishing cities at Grumuntum and Venusia (Venosa); the cities grew and began to draw people from the countryside. Noted Roman poet Orazio Flacco (Horace) was born in Venosa in 65 BC.

216-70 BC: The Punic Wars between the Romans and the Carthaginians brought the theater of war to Lucania with

Hannibal battling near Muro Lucano in 210 BC and Grumentum in 207 BC. Hannibal racked up victories before his defeat in 202 BC, with Rome becoming dominant over the entire Mediterranean region, and demonstrating their naval power as well as land-based military might. Later, the Social Wars brought Spartacus to Lucania in 72 BC.

The Romans established the *latifondi* system of agriculture; large tracts of woods were deforested and planted with grain cultivation, which over time degraded the land quality. Latin replaced the Oscan language, and social structures were Romanized. Rome split into the Western empire and Eastern Byzantium empire (Constantinople). The separation of the empire, decadence, military challenges, and imperial incompetence led to Rome's decline. The suffered territorial losses to the Vandals and the Visigoths, coupled with Germanic expansion until it could no longer retain its empire and "fell" around 450 AD.

BYZANTINES, SARACENS, LOMBARDS 500-1000 AD

In the power vacuum following the fall of Rome, Barbarian invasions ensued. The Goths battled the Byzantines; in 568 the Germanic Lombards invaded Italy, while the Saracens (Arabs) took advantage of the situation in the south and moved in, establishing their presence in Tricarico, Tursi, Castelsaraceno, Pietrapertosa and Pescopagano.

700s – 900s: Byzantine and Lombard monks arrived and established cave churches (rupestrian) in and around Matera; Benedictine-order monasteries were established in several towns around northern Basilicata as well as around Matera.

NORMANS AND SVEVI (SWABIANS)

1041 – 1059: The Normans conquered Melfi, made it a base of military operations and took the majority of southern Italy, effectively ending Byzantine influence in southern Italy. Pope Nicholas II gave the title Duke of Apulia and Calabria to Norman knight Robert Guiscard along with sweeping power for Guiscard's role in chasing the Saracens and Byzantines out of the territory.

1200s: In 1215 Frederick II was crowned Holy Roman Emperor, ushering in Swabian domination. He was called the Stupor Mundi, wonder of the world, for his forward-thinking ideas and the culture he espoused. He established castles in

Basilicata and Puglia, from which many important directives and events took place. In 1231 he issued the Le Costituzioni di Melfi, the first set of modern laws in the Middle Ages. Basilicata had a sort of Renaissance as the Swabian ruler made it an important center of politics and court life. With the death of Frederick II in 1250, conflict over succession and control ensued; Carlo d'Angou came out the winner. Feudalism was ushered in, concentrating land ownership in the hands of a few powerful families and the church, with local inhabitants providing the labor; it was a system that would continue throughout the south until after the unification of Italy in 1860.

ANGEVINS AND ARAGONESI

1300s-1500s: The French Angevins and Spanish Aragonesi feuded over the Kingdom of Naples that covered all of the southern portion of the peninsula. In 1442, the Aragon dynasty took control and brought 200 years of Spanish rule of the Kingdom of Naples (then called Kingdom of the Two Sicilies), eventually losing control to the Bourbon dynasty.

1480s-1700s: Albanian refugees arrived in Basilicata, escaping the persecution of the Ottomans. They established Ginestra, Barile, Maschito, San Costantino Albanese and San Paolo Albanese, towns that continue to carry on the Albanian language, rites and traditions to this day. It was a period of demographic and economic rebound, followed by feudal mismanagement and subjugation that brought increased poverty. In the 1700s there were spotty uprisings that took place and were squelched. In 1799 a backlash started in Avigliano calling for "democratic organization", and spread to other towns. It was harshly put down by the Bourbons. Power struggles continued throughout the centuries with domination passing back and forth between the French and the Spanish Bourbons until 1815.

1805: Napoleon Bonaparte became king of the northern Kingdom of Italy, and took control of the Kingdom of Naples a year later. Napoleon made Joachim Murat (his brother-in-law) the king of Naples, and he shifted the administration capital of the Basilicata district from Matera to Potenza. The Napoleonic code of laws were enacted; many are still in effect today. His dominion lasted until 1815, and the Kingdom of the Two Sicilies (also called Kingdom of Naples) returned to the Bourbons. Infrastructure works and reforms set in motion were undone when Napoleon was overthrown and Murat ousted.

UNIFICATION AND BRIGANTAGGIO, EMIGRATION, AND BEYOND

1861: Northern Italy, Sardinia and parts of central Italy came under the control of the Savoy dynasty, and king Vittorio Emanuele II. Garibaldi had swept through Sicily and southern Italy, displacing the Bourbon king and uniting the peninsula under the House of Savoy. A popular uprising ensued by *briganti*, in protest of the invasion. They were put down ten years later. Land reforms, privatization, trade wars to favor northern industries, undervaluing of agricultural products, and penalties enacted following the *briganti* uprisings all combined to create devastating poverty, inattention to infrastructure and development, and lack of opportunity for southern Italy. The so-called

"Southern problem" started during this period and continues in various forms today.

1880-1920: Millions of southerners left their homeland, disenchanted with the harsh results of the unification and the inability to establish large enough land parcels to make a living or keep their families fed. The massive drain left Italy short of laborers, furthering the infrastructure problems of the south.

1935: Carlo Levi was interred in Basilicata, a political exile for anti-fascist activities. He doctored the townspeople, painted, and chronicled the hard-scrabble life he found in Aliano, one that was a stark contrast to the northern Italian life he knew. In response to his book, Christ Stopped at Eboli, most of the Sassi district in Matera was emptied of inhabitants, who were moved to modern housing in newly-built suburban-type neighborhoods above.

1993: The Sassi of Matera were declared a UNESCO World Heritage Site, bringing funds to restore the district, and attention to the unrecognized place in world history that Matera occupied.

2019: Matera was the Capital of European Culture.

Basilicata By The Numbers

- 562,869: number of residents in Basilicata
- 66,700: population of Potenza, Basilicata's most populated city
- 253: population of San Paolo Albanese, Basilicata's smallest town
- 3,900: size of Basilicata, in square miles
- 41: total length of Basilicata's coastline, in miles
- 92: percentage of Basilicata that comprises mountains or hills
- 87: length of Basilicata from north to south, in air miles
- 2: number of provinces within the region (Potenza and Matera)
- 2: number of seas Basilicata's borders touch (Mediterranean and Ionian)
- 3: number of regions Basilicata borders (Calabria, Campania and Puglia)
- 2: Patron saints – San Gerardo Maiella, born in Muro Lucano, the *santo padronale;* and the Madonna Nera of Viggiano, the region's *protettrice*, the protectoress.

MATERA

THE JEWEL OF BASILICATA

Matera will take your breath away; I dare you not to drop your jaw at the first sight of the undulating jumble of honey-hued buildings that make up the famed Sassi district. Descend into the maze and you'll quickly discover there is so much more to it than you think from that first glimpse at the overlook.

The capital of the province bearing its name, the city itself is captivating, mystical, and oozes antiquity. It is the oldest continuously inhabited city in Europe (and one of the five most ancient in the world). Named a UNESCO World Heritage Site in 1993, it is an architecturally intricate place, much more than a "cave city" as many articles suggest: it has every epoch of history incised in the tufa stone and visible in the sinewy passageways. The ancient streets, worn smooth from the centuries, hide many treasures, and there are hidden courtyards, mysterious corners, and a complicated street system where pedestrian lanes pass over rooftops with chimneys sticking right through from the houses below.

First, an orientation. There are four districts to Matera. **The Sassi** district is the soul of Matera, the ancient and unique city occupying the *gravina* gorge; it is built onto, into, and out of the tufa rock in an incredibly complex design. Indeed, the word *sassi* means rocks. The cliff is pocked by natural caves that were used as dwellings in the Bronze Age, and have been inhabited ever since. There are two sections: the **Sasso Caveoso** is the less-developed section, curving and conforming to the shape of the cliff; **Sasso Barisano** is the area that grew and developed as the city blossomed, where thousands of homes were constructed and excavated to become a truly mind-boggling city. **The Civita** is the highest point and level area where the cathedral, civic buildings, and noble palaces were built. Its center had been Piazza Sedile. The Civita had previously been protected by walls. **The Centro**, also known as the **Piano**, is the pulsing heart of the city, an area added as the population increased in the 1700s. With wider spaces, piazzas, and palaces, it wraps around the edge of the Sassi and Civita. **The New Town** is the vast sprawl built in the postwar era when the Sassi were declared unfit for habitation and the population forcibly moved to newer and "better" homes.

The identity of Matera is its unusual Sassi. The famed caves were inhabited in prehistoric times, then for centuries by Byzantine and Benedictine monks who carved out homes in the tufa rock and transformed primitive caves into color-coated churches, slathered in decorative frescoes. There are more than 150 rock churches scattered on both sides of the ravine; the most impressive is the Crypt of Original Sin (#3). In the "upper city" starting in the 900s, a castle and medieval walls were built, along with churches and homes. The city of the Middle Ages prospered. Winemaking was an important industry, and the caves of the Sassi offered ideal conditions for the fermentation and storage. As the population grew, they burst out of the walls, further and further down the cliff, creating unique dwelling spaces by building solid-block houses right onto the precipice, using the edifice below as the foundation for the one above. The Sassi expanded until it practically filled the cliff wall with tufa-stone homes, tucking into the folds of the steep terrain. A complicated system of canals and cisterns was developed to provide water to the Sassi. Agriculture was practiced on the plains, the farmers returning to their homes in the Sassi at night. In the 1700s, folks again looked upward and starting building *palazzi* and more spacious housing on the Piano above. Wars, economic decline, and political neglect had caused the Sassi to be reduced to such squalor, at least in parts, that it was declared the "shame of Italy" after Carlo Levi's famous book, Christ Stopped at Eboli (#11) drew attention to the decay. The Sassi were forcibly emptied and the occupants relocated to the modern concrete dwellings elsewhere.

Fortunately, the history and timeless beauty of the Sassi led to UNESCO World Heritage Site status in 1993, and they were rehabilitated, repopulated, and reborn. Like a desert flower, it has bloomed among the thorns of its hardscrabble history and was named European Capital of Culture in 2019. The best way to really see the Sassi is with a guide. (See: www.discovery-matera.it; www.materatours.net; www.materacitytour.it for English guides.)

There is so much to see here that I could write a 52 Things book dedicated solely to Matera. The following pages offer some highlights and experiences, but you should also meander and got lost in the labyrinth of streets of the Sassi; there are delights to be found there. Marvel at the intricacy of this place. You'll walk down, then up, then down, then…well, a lot of walking. You can get a basic overview with a cute **Ape Tour** (AH-pay), but as there are only two streets for cars in the Sassi, that is limited (but it is a lot of fun.) The lower road, **Via Madonna della Virtu** lets you see the ravine on both sides. **Piazza San Pietro Caveoso** is a dramatic corner suspended over the ravine, with three churches in a few feet of each other. **San Pietro church** grips the lip of the cliff, while the 13th century **Santa Maria de Idris** is excavated into the rocky spire that looms above, with a fresco-festooned **crypt of San Giovanni** below it, both marvels of ingenuity and mystical beauty. The **Convicinio di Sant'Antonio** in Sasso Caveoso is a series of chambers traversed by plank walkways, connecting ancient cave churches, crypts and wine cantinas that were hewn into the hillside. You'll find plenty of excellent eateries sprinkled around the Sassi.

In the **Civita** district, don't miss the **cathedral,** a majestic Romanesque jewel that underwent a ten-year restoration. Built in the 1200s, it is the defining landmark to Matera's low-profile skyline and the highest point of town. It is the most ornately-adorned church in Basilicata, festooned with gilding and lavish baroque;

it also holds the city's most prized possession, the painting of La Bruna. The Madonna della Bruna is the patron saint; her statue is taken in a solemn procession every July 2, that then turns into a riotous (fun) affair.

In the **Piano** district, the museum in the **Palazzo Lanfranchi** has a cache of paintings by Carlo Levi, who was a political exile in Basilicata during the Fascist era. His epic Lucania '61 is striking. There are many other works of regional art worth seeing here. The **Chiesa del Purgatorio** is macabrely adorned with dozens of skulls and skeletons. The interior is frosted in neo-baroque style. After a trip to Purgatory, commune with the angels at **I Vizi degli Angeli**, the best gelateria in Matera, in Via Ridola.

But onward; in the following pages I take you into the caves, and beyond.

1. Swim In A Cave
(And Sleep In One, Too!)

While Matera seems like a prehistoric rock city, there was actually a complex overall architectural plan to build a city of this size into the folds of the rocky slope. An important part of this urban scheme included a system of cisterns and canals to provide water to the different districts, called *vicinati*.

La Locanda di San Martino Hotel e Antiche Termae Romane has transformed one of those cisterns and accompanying channels into a splendid subterranean swimming pool and spa, so you can enjoy some of Matera's history while soaking and blissing out. The hotel and spa have played on the Roman rite of ritual baths to provide a wellness circuit of different temperatures, a pool with thumping (read: stress-relieving) hydro-massage jets, steam and dry saunas, and plays of light "for sensory relaxation" they say.

You can add in a massage or facial, with a choice – foot massage, or just legs, for example, perfect if you've been out hiking or spent the whole day trekking the ups and downs of the Sassi. Or opt for a regular body massage with soothing lavender oil or energizing rosemary-mint oils.

But really, the highlight is the underground pool and Roman spa circuit that takes you through those channels and chambers. If you're not a guest at the hotel, you can still reserve to use the Termae (reserve online.)

The hotel itself is nicely done and one of Matera's most notable, with a choice of rooms in the cave portions or in the external built-out parts of the building for those who want a window on the rocky world outside (or maybe you're like me and simply want natural light streaming in). There are terraces, and the location is quiet, down at the bottom of the Sassi.

Of course, there are plenty of other hotels that offer cave rooms, at all price points. I'm partial to **Residence San Giorgio**, as the young and enthusiastic owners were among the first to open a hotel in the Sassi, and we watched them renovate and open new sections a bit at a time, doing all the work themselves (with help from friends). It is a family-owned labor-of-love kind of place, and they'll give you a warm welcome and help you get oriented. Some rooms are cave suites while others are in the historic built-out sections, townhouse style. All have a kitchenette, and plenty of space, along with great atmosphere, and you can hear musical notes wafting down from the conservatory above (#2). (Ask them to show you the *cisterna*!)

Corte San Pietro and **Le Dimore dell'Idris** are two properties in the bottom of the Sassi near the church of Idris, also restored by local families, though each has a different style, with Le Dimore dell'Idris taking a more modern approach to the furnishings (but not going to the extreme "boutique modern" that usually means "generically the same and void of character"). No, they have artist-designed headboards, slick contemporary bathrooms and some high-tech features while keeping the cave ambiance. (When you see it, it will make more sense.) Corte San Pietro is on a quiet courtyard with rooms opening onto it, keeps things more rustic but the beds are super-comfy. Again, service is customer-focused and welcoming. There are many, many options in the Sassi, though, so go ahead and sleep in a cave. When in Matera…

2. Hear The Sound Of Music In Matera

In the heart of Matera's Civita sits the nearly-enclosed **Piazza del Sedile**, sunning on the level stripe that divides the Sasso Barisano from the Sasso Caveoso. Once-upon-a-time it was named Piazza Grande, because, well, it was. Piazza Grande was the heart of Matera, where in the 1500s the Palazzo del Sedile served as city hall, where artisan workshops and civic life mingled.

Around the corner is Piazza San Francesco with its ornate baroque church that is not only a fave with Materani weddings, it is also the keeper of the Madonna della Bruna statue that gets taken for a processional ride in a lavishly-decorated cart every July 2.

But back to the Sedile Square, where the former *palazzo* is now the headquarters of a prestigious music school, the Conservatorio di Musica Statale. At any given hour of the day you'll hear strains of classical violin, jazz piano or lively flute wafting throughout the piazza and the street running at its end towards the cathedral. Practice sessions and classrooms keep the notes flowing all day long from a building on the piazza and a former palazzo on Via Duomo.

The Palazzo del Sedile with its slightly askew bell tower bears a frescoed portico that once held court gatherings when Matera was part of the Kingdom of Naples. It was built in 1540 but given a facelift in the mid-1700s when it was enlarged. The towers show a clock and a meridian, and the four statues placed in niches represent the cardinal virtues. Those on top between the towers are the Madonna Bruna, Matera's protectress, and Sant'Eustachio, the city's patron saint.

The music conservatory was established in 1965 and named for local composer Egidio Romualdo Duni. It was the first in the region and remains the most prestigious in the area. Besides the music you'll hear from the classrooms, the school organizes regular concerts in the Auditorium Gervasio, located right here under Piazza Sedile, and with the non-profit Orchestra Magna Grecia that plays throughout the city and province.

The music doesn't stop here, though. Matera is also known for its love of jazz, with regular gigs at Palazzo Lanfranchi, which also houses the fabulous Lanfranchi Museum, and the cave-theater called Casa Cava. The Onyx Jazz Club organizes the concert series, called Gezziamoci (meaning, let's jazz). Look for their schedule if you're an enthusiast; they're really high caliber.

Also on the music front, if you're here in summer and it's your lucky day, there may be a concert in the evocative Cava del Sole, a music venue placed inside one of the former stone quarries. It may sound strange, but the acoustics are excellent and the setting is superb.

The Piazza del Sedile is the literal middle ground between the two sections of the Sassi: from the palazzo's left, a staircase descends into Sasso Caveoso; at the opposite end if the square is the low arch, Arco Sant'Antonio, below which lies the Sasso Barisano. This is still the central point of Matera. So, sit for a spell, enjoy a beverage or a pizza…and the sound of music.

More Information: Orchestra Magna Grecia
http://www.orchestramagnagrecia.info
Onyx Jazz Club
https://www.onyxjazzclub.com/?lang=en (English)

3. MATERA

REFLECT AT THE SISTINE CHAPEL OF THE SOUTH

A true masterpiece of detailed angelic artwork isn't held in a museum, or even a cathedral, but in a cave. This is Matera, after all. The Crypt of Original Sin (Cripta del Peccato Originale in Italian) is a *chiesa rupestre*, or cave church, and the paintings frescoed on the walls are so impressive that the grotto is called "The Sistine Chapel of the South." Or, more specifically, the Sistine Chapel of rupestrian churches.

This cave almost fell into total oblivion. It is not in the city but about nine miles outside of Matera along the *gravina* in the area called Petrapenta, a pocked rocky escarpment that slices the landscape. The story goes that a pair of shepherds had been using various caves in the area for their sheep. One evening as darkness was falling one of them with his grandson located this particular grotto and closed the animals in for the night. When they returned in the morning, they were certainly surprised to find a host of saints looking at them from the walls!

It was rediscovered in May, 1963 and dubbed The Grotto of a Hundred Saints. But even then, it was not well known or considered an attraction. Over another couple of decades, the paintings were at risk of being lost due to climate, water, lichen and mold, and so a highly specialized restoration took place with geological, scientific, biology and artistic experts. They thankfully salvaged these delightful paintings.

What's so special about it? Well, that it has survived at all is quite a feat! That the details of the frescoes are still so vivid after more than a millennium is stunning. The crypt isn't a crypt in the sense you may think, by the way, in that it was never a burial chamber. It was a church for an order of Benedictine monks. The devotional art was painted by an artist known only as The Flower Painter of Matera.

Its current name comes from one of the paintings –that indelible scene from Genesis of Adam, Eve, the serpent and the fruit – the original sin. Like the Sistine Chapel, there is a painting of the Creation, much of it still distinguishable but sadly a good portion of it was lost to the elements. There are three niches that contain the Apostles, the Virgin Mary, and the Archangels. All of the frescoes are intertwined with delicate flowers; the artist had a real affinity for them, hence his name.

There are many rupestrian churches in Matera, embedded in the perforated ravine walls facing the city, but this one is by far the most spectacular, so I highly recommend a visit. To do so, you must reserve online or go with a local guide. If you have a car, you'll find the *Cripta del Peccato Originale* at the Dragone farm.

The Dragone family has owned the land for generations but donated the grotto to the Fondazione Zetema so this gem could be available to the public. The ***famiglia* Dragone** produce some tasty wines, though, so you may want to stop by while you're here.

Information and reservations:
www.criptadelpeccatooriginale.it
Dragone Winery: https://dragonevini.com

4. GET INTO SOME METAL ROCK IN MATERA

With the city's prime attraction and ancient city called the Sassi, it's obvious that rocks will be involved. But it is taken to a different level at La Palomba, one of Matera's most overlooked spots just outside town. The contemporary open-air art gallery is situated in the old stone quarry where the tufa was extracted to build the city, its sheer walls striped with the cut lines.

Instead of leaving a desolate scar, it's decorated with whimsical and heart-warming metal and rock sculptures by Antonio Paradiso and other artists. The breezes through the grass and (sometimes) nearby sheep bells are all you're likely to hear; we've rarely seen other people about, despite its free admission and fanciful works.

La Palomba was first an ancient Neolithic settlement where parts of a megalithic wall are still on display. The art part of it sits within a larger, extensive *parco archeologico storico naturale*, which is to natural say, an archeological and natural history park, so do feel free to wander the paths up and around to see some of those remains. By the way, it gets its name from the 16th century church up among the trees above the quarry, Santuario di Santa Maria della Palomba.

But back to the metal rock – the non-profit gallery is deemed an "anthropological art park." You can read whatever you want into that, and into the works themselves. The forged metal and carved stone sculptures are thought-provoking, whimsical, abstract and uplifting. Birds are a recurring theme, in keeping with the *palomba* name (Spanish for dove). Some tall tubular steel and carved stone pieces highlight that bird, and it shows up in many other works, too. The Squashed Bug is one you can't miss, and it's sure to make you smile.

Two works stand out, and are especially poignant for us American visitors. Following 9/11 the Port Authority launched a project to bring beauty from the ashes and re-use some of the steel material from Ground Zero in artwork worldwide. Of the 9,000 artists who applied, Antonio Paradiso was one of about 40 selected; he received 20 tons of steel from Hangar 17. With it, he created two vastly different pieces. The first is the Global Last Supper, a spectral gathering of Christ and the apostles that kept the twisted and burned metal in its stark forms. A steel fragment serves as the table. It is humble and haunting at the same time.

The other is Ascension, a metal box balancing on its tip with laser-cut doves; it is both light-hearted and precarious, an uplifting tribute where the birds represent the souls of the victims of that tragic day. The cut-out doves are placed in yet another work.

This is a place of quiet contemplation, and of thought-provoking artwork, as well as of archeological significance. No wonder the founding artist refers to it as an anthropological Peace Park. The acoustics are so astounding near the walls that summer concerts are sometimes held here. It's a great place for a quiet picnic; grab something from La Latteria or a *paninoteca* in town and hike up to enjoy the scene from above. The breeze and birds sing to you; it may not be a metal-rock tune, but then the whole park satisfies that theme.

More information: http://www.parcosculturalapalomba.it

While You're Here

The Santuario Santa Maria della Palomba is a 16th century church rife with fine frescoes and worth a visit. A more ancient *chiesa rupestre* is found below, accessibly from the presbytery, which you shouldn't miss.

Also, just past the Parco La Palomba is a road that leads to the Belvedere at the Parco della Murgia, and you should take that turn-off from the Via Appia SS7 because it leads you to a marvelous panoramic view across the Gravina to see how Matera's extensive Sassi is tucked into all the folds of the ravine. You can also see the course of the city's development as you sweep your eyes from left –the Sassi Caveosi- to the right, where the Sassi Barisano is more built up and extensive; and the Civita' above, easily identified by the cathedral's tower. The *centro* stands behind it.

5. Do Some Carbo-Loading In Matera

This is no place for those low-carb diets! Not. At. All. Matera doesn't just produce good bread; they produce a bread so sublime it has special recognitions from Slow Food, and the coveted IGP status as a protected product.

At the heart of its excellence is the flour: double-ground *semola*, the same hard-durum wheat flour used to make those *cavatelli* and *orecchiette* pastas. The IGP designation lays out strict guidelines including the grain used –it must be the heritage Capelli or Duro Lucano variety, grown locally; additional directives spell out the milling, the yeast starter (fruit-based), the form of the loaf, and the baking, which is done in a wood-burning oven only.

One taste tells it all – the crunchy crust and soft straw-colored interior is what all bread ought to be. Those lumpy loaves may look weird, but they sure are delicious! This bread carries on an unbroken centuries-long tradition. The secret to good bread was always based on two important elements: the women who knew how to make the dough, and the *fornaio* who knew how to bake it just right. A woman made her family's dough weekly and carried it on a board, often balanced on her head, to the communal bread oven. She stamped it with a carved *timbro di pane*, bread stamp, which marked hers with a unique emblem, so she and the baker knew which loaves were hers when she came back for them. You can still find rustic *timbri di pane* in some of the shops; they make a very special and unique souvenir.

The baker, for his part, had to maintain the wood-fired oven at just the right temperature all day to evenly bake the bread. He would make three cuts in the top before baking it, giving it the strange form. The cuts were said to represent the Father, Son and Holy Spirit. Which means Matera's bread really is heavenly.

The carbs don't stop with the bread, though; there's the pasta (obvious), the pizza (duh) but also soft *focaccia* with tons of topping options, and taste-popping *panzerotti*, which are like miniature calzones that are fried. Oh yeah. Other local goodies? *Pucce* (POO-chay) is a pita-like bread for sandwiches; *taralli* crisp, crumbly ring-shaped crackers; and *friselle* -crunchy donut-shaped dried bread-biscuits that are rehydrated and topped with tomatoes and onions. You should definitely lay on the carbs and try them all. When in Matera, after all.

Try: **Panificio Cifarelli**, via San Francesco, 13; or **Casa del Pane**, Piazza Vittorio Veneto.

6. Drink With The Stars In Bernalda

I'm not talking about celestial sightings like in Anzi (#39); this star gazing is more in the Rodeo Drive caliber. Small it may be, but Bernalda has a place in the film and music galaxy where the glitterati go to unwind. That's because Francis Ford Coppola made a return to his roots, and brought his Hollywood posse with him.

Coppola's grandfather Agostino never forgot his hometown, always referring to it as *"Bernalda bella,"* creating a sort of fairytale mystique about the place that he passed on to his grandson. Francis bought the Palazzo Margherita in 2004 and turned it into a ritzy retreat for A-list friends and regular folks who can shell out to enter the inner sanctum. Tarantino, De Niro, Stallone, George Lucas, Johnny Depp, to name-drop a few, show up from time to time. As does Coppola, who, the Bernaldesi say, "just acts like one of us." Except that he and his friends arrive by helicopter, which lands at the town's soccer stadium.

The palace of painted frescoes, palatial rooms, and hidden cloister-like garden are what you'd expect from a swanky hotel, but even more –this one includes a private screening room, giving the term movie-on-demand real meaning. The nine suites were decorated with the exacting detail that Coppola gives to his films, each one with a different theme, with one set aside for his own use. The dreamy garden is protected by the Italian Cultural Heritage Department, and was the setting for Sophia Coppola's marriage to musician Thomas Mars. It all feels homey and lavish at the same time. If you can get in the door, that is. The place is so elite that it is unmarked by any signs and only those with a reservation can pass through the heavy greyish gateway.

That doesn't mean you can't rub elbows with the stars, though, because the hotel's Cinecittà Bar is open to the public. Walk inside and sit down surrounded by actors amidst the star-studded walls. Photos of actors and directors are the primary décor of the place, named for the prominent Italian movie studio in Rome. I like that it is cozy yet classy, the staff is always friendly, and a glass of wine doesn't set me back much more than any ordinary bar (though, let's face it, they could price gouge if they wanted to). The *aperitivo* comes with a nice assortment of snacks (called *stuzzicchini* –STOOT-sc-kcc-nee) to nibble on while sipping and chatting and enjoying the ambiance. I prefer to be at the outside umbrella-topped tables to watch the people parade of Bernaldesi and the tables of older gents across the street playing cards. It's also a good spot for a bit of voyeurism: you can watch as dark-tinted, chauffeur-driven cars arrive and wait for the gates to opened to the inner realm. Oh, is that Leo Di Caprio?

While Cinecittà is also billed as a bistrot, we only come for drinks rather than meals, because really it is primarily a bar. There are some excellent eateries here in Bernalda to enjoy, but an *aperitivo* in this pretty galaxy is a nice way to start the evening.

While You're Here – Take a walk through the old town of Bernalda with its tight web of streets culminating at the castle and church, with a panoramic overlook and a great restaurant with a view, Ristorante alle Porte. If you really want to go local, have dinner at a *braceria*, a local fave that combines butcher shop by day with grill by night. You choose the meats from the counter and they cook them for you over a fire. The real specialty here is **carne di cavallo** (horse meat) which some *bracerie* do exclusively, while others offer a variety of meats.

7. Get Philosophical In Metaponto

Long before the Romans came, the Greeks arrived on the coastal plains along the Ionian Sea, bringing their advanced culture and way of life. The fertile land is sliced with rivers and represents the only flat plain in the region, and today it is a hothouse of fruit and vegetable cultivation. The strawberries you buy in Rome were probably grown near Metaponto.

But in the 8th century BC, it was an outpost colony of Greece that became a flourishing city and among the most important of Magna Graecia. It was endowed with temples and protective walls and gained political and economic strength. They minted money; the local coins bore a wheat head, demonstrating its value as an agricultural colony. It also saw some of history's big names pass through its streets.

Its most illustrious resident was the philosopher and mathematician Pythagoras, who sought refuge in Metaponto after being driven out of Crotone in the 6th century BC.

Pythagoras and his followers settled in here and he continued the philosophical education he had started in Crotone to pass on his theories and wisdom. His school was a monastic-style commune where he imparted his observations on math, music and astronomy to his students, and liberally allowed women followers. He believed all things were made of numbers and is credited with breakthroughs such as the Pythagorean theorem, the theory of proportions, and the theory that music was tied to numbers.

His ideas influenced Copernicus, Johannes Kepler, and Isaac Newton, and were mentioned by Dante; his theories on mathematical perfection also influenced ancient Greek art, and later Roman art and architecture. It is said that Porta Maggiore Basilica, built during the reign of Nero, and the Pantheon were constructed using Pythagorean numerology. Was Pythagoras's wisdom at work several millennia later in Acerenza? (#51). Some say yes.

He died here around 490 BC. His house and school were likely adjacent to the Temple of Hera; the temple is a sight to behold and one you shouldn't miss. Called the Tavole Palatine, the 15 Doric columns stand as witness to the florid community that existed here so many thousands of years ago.

Ancient Metaponto sided against Rome in the Battle of Eraclea in 280 BC, and was punished. Many fled to Pisticci and Ginosa. When the city gave shelter to Hannibal and his troops in 207 BC, the Romans had enough and destroyed Metapontum. It is said the *castrum romano* was built from the ruins to house the Roman troops. Spartacus and his rebels met no opposition and encamped here for a winter between 72 and 73 BC, and according to Plutarch, garnered Lucani recruits.

The stones from the Greek buildings were recycled by the Romans and later settlers, but the site is a rarity in Italy –no medieval buildings were constructed over top of the ancient structures. That means that archeologists were able to map the entire ancient urban plan; so, while little remains standing, the Parco Archeologico di Metaponto bears the outlines of the theater, other temples and buildings.

The National Archeology Museum holds the artifacts that were found here and around Pisticci, so definitely go and gander at the mind-boggling array of ceramics, sculptures crockery, and coins.

My advice is to time your visit to end at the Tavole Palatine in the late afternoon; there is something truly mystical here at sunset. Maybe the breeze and wildflowers still exude the ancient philosophical wisdom of Pythagoras and his followers? Or maybe the beauty with diffused colored light just makes one think deep thoughts.

More information: www.basilicataturistica.it

8. Go To "That Town" That Nobody Names

If you want to see a panic reaction from a Lucanian, say the word "Colobraro" and stand back. They'll either cross themselves or thrust their hands downward in an inverted Texas longhorn gesture to ward off any bad karma your utterance may have spun into the air, while exclaiming emphatically, "NON SI NOMINA!" (You don't say that!) That's because Colobraro has a reputation as the unluckiest town in Italy. It is so afflicted, in fact, that nobody utters its name; they merely refer to it as "*quel paese*," or, 'that town', lest the Colobraro curse rub off.

It doesn't seem so direful when you arrive. Strapped atop a steep bluff, the vertiginous position gives off views of the canyon-striped landscape and distant mountains, looking a lot like the scenery of an old Western movie. In town, there are postage stamp piazzas and huddled houses intertwined by narrow alley-streets. It looks so pleasant and respectable. But…does something calamitous lurk among those lanes?

The town's unfortunate reputation earned urban legend status before the second world war. The ill-repute stems from a blend of documented facts and myth that took hold and expanded, spreading the word of the town's misfortune. In the 1930s a politician passionately pleaded his case and at the end of the assembly declared, "If I'm not telling the truth, may the chandelier fall on me!" Which it did, injuring not just the magistrate but a few others, as well.

Ernesto De Martino, a Neapolitan anthropologist who penned a book about southern superstitions and magic, studied the Colobraro phenomenon in the '50s, documenting and confirming the unlucky episodes that seemed to plague the place. Whether the bad aura was cast off in the past several years or not, visitors will see that the residents definitely have a good sense of humor and are able to joke about their bad rep.

They have turned the tide on their dubious reputation by taking the bad bull by the horns, so to speak, and poking fun at it with a summer show. They've cleverly played on their underdog status to bring tourists to town and promote the place, while enhancing the folkloric traditions of the region. This is a magic-steeped country after all, and the Colobraro show expands on that. Back in the day, each town used to have a "diviner" or seer –some still do. (Another town in the region has a festival dedicated to that aspect, called La Notte della Magia, or the night of magic, in Albano di Lucania.)

Colobraro puts on the self-deprecatory itinerate show in the streets of town every Tuesday and Friday in August.

If you can't come for the show, that's okay. The town is perfectly friendly and the views from up there, high above the Valle del Sinni, extend over the valley and across miles of the strange *calanchi* canyon formations to the mountains beyond. A museum up at the top part of town is one of the better rural life museums I've seen, demonstrating how wool spinning and fabrics were a major industry in Colobraro in the past, along with other displays.

But really, it's all about the notoriety. So, if you want to tempt fate, go to "that town" and defy the naysayers…if you dare.

9. Meet The Sea Turtles In Policoro

The Ionian shore with its flat unbroken lengths of golden sand is the polar opposite of Maratea's rocky, cove-studded coast (#16) and draws families who like the shallow water and easy access. The beaches here also attract sea turtles that come to nest and, since 2008, have seen an increase in hatchings, thanks to the efforts of the World Wildlife Fund's Oasi di Policoro and its turtle protection program.

The nature reserve is known by various names –Bosco di Pantano, WWF Herekleia, and WWF Policoro. The area is left entirely in its natural state, and the forest that runs along the beach is among of the last coastal plain forests in Italy.

The park covers a mix of wetland, woods and coastal sands between the Sinni and Agri Rivers, a unique landscape with limited access and no development allowed, giving the flora and fauna a chance to thrive. There are pines and poplars, scrub oaks and junipers, along with rockrose, sea lilies, wild licorice, and the distinct fragrant *macchia* of wild rosemary, bay, and myrtle. The reserve attracts migratory birds such as egrets and herons, along with badgers and martens that also call the woods home.

But it is the sea turtle program that's the star. Here they monitor the nests, identify and protect areas ideal for nesting, cure sick and injured turtles, and more. The Policoro WWF program takes in the entire Ionian coast from Taranto to Calabria's tip and is carried out in conjunction with the University of Calabria. While the emergence of the baby turtles usually occurs at night, sometimes it happens in the daylight and, with safe distance viewing to not confuse the little creatures, it's a real thrill to watch them crawl to the sea. By the way, did you know that baby turtles are born with a carbuncle, a temporary tooth to break out of the egg? It can take days to break free; then the hatchlings –as many as 60 or more at once-use their innate honing to find the sea. Fascinating! The species found here is the C*aretta caretta*, which is endangered, but the program's success is encouraging for their future.

A visit to the WWF Oasi d Policoro for a tour and a bit of nature will surely bring you face-to-face with a *tartaruga* in their rescue program's turtle care facility. While you can't swim at the WWF center, the beaches of Marina di Pisticci have seen hatchings, too. It's rare but you may just catch a glimpse of *tartarughe* swimming off shore, or evidence of a female making her nest in the sand. With or without an "in the wild" turtle sighting, you can hit the soft, sandy beach for a bit of sun and surf.

More information:
https://www.wwf.it/tartarugamarina (Italian)

Check hours and schedule a tour of the Oasi Herakleia Policoro: http://www.oasiwwfpolicoro.net

Beaches to check out at Marina di Pisticci: My favorites are Lido La Spiaggetta and Lido Natura. Next to both of them are huge swaths of free beach, so you can walk a little and find solitude (and maybe, just maybe, a turtle sighting).

10. SEARCH FOR GHOSTS IN A REAL, LIVE (UM) GHOST TOWN

The first sight of Craco is dramatic – a stone town rising from a jagged rock pinnacle 1,200 feet above the strange lunar-like canyon formations and valley below it. The outline of the town staggering up the hill to the Norman tower at the summit is a vision, until you get closer and see the caved-in roofs and yawning windows that display the loneliness of the place. It looks like something from a ghostly Gothic novel or carefully constructed movie set. Craco, you see, is dead, a ghost town.

Walk around it and you'll see it was once rather grand, with a wide street up to a piazza, studded by *palazzi* with pretty portals, ornate wrought-iron balconies, an impressive church. Craco was once brimming with life, albeit a precarious one. The area's peculiar clay and hydraulic situation left it prone to landslides. They built a retaining wall and bridge. The land continued to move. In 1959, an unusually heavy rain left all the surrounding areas with a sinking feeling (literally) -and the bridge moved while houses cracked. That made them really start to worry. When the situation repeated in 1963, it became more critical and people decided maybe they should move, before their houses did, and the concrete new town of Craco Peschiera was built. By 1971, the town was really sliding, a new wall sunk by two meters, and the rest of the hold-out residents were forced to skedaddle. An earthquake in 1980 rattled any last hope they may have had about returning to the hilltop town. Mother Nature, it seemed, had it in for poor Craco.

Now a ghost town, Craco, oddly and ironically, is more alive as a tourist destination than the depressing new town below, its eerily empty streets now an attraction. It's also occasionally used as a film set: Christ Stopped at Eboli, The Passion of the Christ, Basilicata Coast to Coast and Quantum of Solace all filmed scenes here, among others. You can visit Craco yourself and search for ghosts among the ruins. But beware: locals and visitors alike have reported feeling sudden chills and seeing fleeting shadows, without explanation, so it really may be an *actual* ghost's town. (Freaked out yet?)

The only way to visit is on a tour -with a guide and a helmet. The tour starts in the old monastery dedicated to San Pietro just below, near the cemetery where an interactive museum provides information and contrasting before-and-after photos. The monastery itself helps you see what Craco was like before all its troubles. Then a guide takes your through to see the old yet attractive abandonment. Blue was a recurring color here, painted in rooms and on doors, thought to ward off evil spirits. Apparently, it didn't work. The tour goes up, up, up to the Norman tower, where there are gorgeous views, glorious silence and a sense of peace…except for a ghost or two.

Tours run regularly from 9:30 AM until dusk but advance reservations are only for groups. The check-in point is at the Mediateca Comunale in Via Sant'Angelo (follow the signs), just beyond the abandoned city. The Monastero di San Pietro with the museum is open from 9:30 AM until 4:00 PM. Craco by Night tours can be organized if you have a small group, by reservation. If you want to ensure an English-language tour, contact them in advance by sending an email to international@cracomuseum.eu.

More information: https://www.cracomuseum.eu

11. Follow The Footsteps of an Exiled Rebel in Aliano

Aliano seems to bask in its infamy. Seventy-some years ago it had been a typical peasant village in remote southern Basilicata, scraping to survive, ignored and derided by the central government. It would have remained hidden and forgotten had it not been paid a visit by destiny.

When the Mussolini government wanted to silence the anti-fascist political writings and rabble-rousings of a Jewish doctor named Carlo Levi, it could think of no punishment more severe than banishment from his northern city of Torino to the hinterlands of Basilicata. Here amidst the lunar-like hills far from any city, it seemed as far away as the moon; modern communications and northern news filtered slowly, so Levi and his inflammatory activism would be safely out of their dictatorial hair.

Levi arrived in Aliano to find an abject poverty in stark contrast of his prosperous north, which seemed a different world. The remote locale was neglected and remained outside of time while resources were focused on northern industrial technologies and interests. Levi spent his two years of political exile acting as town physician while painting local scenes and characters and taking detailed journalistic notes which he would use to write his well-known book, Christ Stopped at Eboli. From his house on the edge of the village, Levi observed, interacted with, and painted the lives, hardships, and contrasts of a place within his country that was foreign to him.

When he was released from his house arrest, Levi penned his most famous work, which shed light on the political, economic and social disparity of the south, and would eventually bring attention and change to the region. And the town of Aliano couldn't have been more grateful.

Today, Aliano is still small and somewhat remote, but the appearance, well-being and status are quite different thanks in large part to Levi, whose works live on there. The town has been declared a Literary Park, and travelers come from around the world to walk in his footsteps. Plaques are affixed to buildings with quotes in Levi's words as he had described each landmark, so visitors can tour the town and see it through his eyes –and their own at the same time.

The grateful town pays homage to their famous guest with many places named in his honor- a street, a piazza, a coffee bar, a restaurant. A statue of him stands at the entrance to Aliano. It was Levi's request to be buried here, and his grave lies in a panoramic spot in the cemetery above town, his tomb sprinkled with pebbles. Enjoy the view up there of olive groves, canyon-riddled landscapes, and distant mountains.

The house of Levi's interment has been turned into a museum and many of his paintings are on display in the Pinacoteca (art gallery) and you shouldn't miss either of them. The Casa *museo* has been left as it was in 1936, to give visitors a faithful sense of it; an evocative video blends Levi's words and art with photos and history to bring it all to life (available in English, too). The Pinacoteca is a well-curated collection of Levi's artworks, put together and displayed in an excellent sequence to see the development of his artistic styles and themes. To visit, you'll have to start at the visitor's office. It is just past Piazza Garibaldi as you head towards town, on the right side. It appears closed, but go ahead and open the door, as there is usually someone there. If not, call (+39) 0835 568529. There are set hours for the tours (11:30 AM and 4:30 PM in winter; 5:30 PM in summer) but if miss them the docents will open the two museums for you. If you want to set up tours in advance, the easiest way is through the website: www.parcolevi.it/contatti

While You're Here...

You've come this far, enjoy a fabulous lunch and the other sights.

There are panoramic overlooks sprinkled around town, to take in the vast territory of green hills and so-called badlands. Cross the bridge from the older part of town to the "newer" where you really get a view of the gullies. If you like to hike, there are marked trails that wander those canyons. There is information on www.parcolevi.it under *Percorsi* (Italian only).

The Seer's House. Across from the town hall on Piazza Garibaldi is *La Casa con gli Occhi* – the house with eyes. Which, indeed, seems to be a face with eyes. One legend says it once belonged to a seer, who had it built that way to ward off any "evil eye" curses someone might try to throw her way. Magic was (and remains) a feature of country life in these parts.

More Information: www.parcolevi.it (only Italian).

12. Drink To Your Digestion

If you've traveled to Italy, you've surely noticed that dining has a pre-determined order. Meals are divided into proper courses, starting with *aperitivi* (drinks), on to the *antipasto* (the "pre-meal" appetizer), then the *primo*, *secondo*, vegetable, dessert, and ritual *caffe'*. But it's not just the order of things that matter: there is another time-honored ritual called the *digestivo*. You see, everything hinges on you being able to properly digest that fabulous meal you just enjoyed.

Digestivi are strong alcoholic herbal brews extracted from a variety of herbs and spices. Because the herbs are mostly bitter, they are called amaro, and so they are frequently highly sugared to make them more palatable. Amari (plural) are popular and each region has its preferred tonic. Some are super-blends of various herbs and plants, like our own home-grown and nationally popular Amaro Lucano, which is made from a secret selection of 30 herbs and spices. (Get it? Amaro *Lucano*?) Made in Basilicata, baby!

It all started in pretty Pisticci when a pastry chef with a passion for herbal remedies took to the garden in search of the perfect liqueur. Pasquale Vena didn't even start out to be a pastry chef. He had gone to Naples with his brother, ready to board a ship to America to find his fortune, but it found him instead, with an internship in a pastry shop in Napoli, a city known for its sweets. He returned home and opened his *biscottificio* (cookie bakery). And then the herbal experimentation began.

He obviously hit on the perfect combo for his liqueur and it took off quickly, reaching the royal House of Savoy. The king so enjoyed it that he knighted Pasquale Vena for his ingenious digestive and so even today the bottles carry "Cav. Pasquale Vena" on the neck, "cav" for "*cavaliere*" meaning knight, or, the equivalent of England's "Sir Pasquale". Today, the fourth generation is at the helm, and with their new factory, they can produce more than 4 million bottles a year, and have added other digestive liqueurs, all locally-based, like licorice, *limoncello*, and *caffè*. The coffee cordial, as it is called, for its part, has roots in the small hill town of Laurenzana, and was popularized by a local distillery, Laraia, who sold the recipe to the Vena family. So, it's all still sort of in the Lucania famiglia.

Lucano Essenza – The Immersive Experience. Yes, the Lucano brand may bear a peasant woman on the label but they're hip to the times and have a techy multi-media museum that is also billed as multi-sensory (ahem, meaning you get to taste the stuff). The displays walk you through some of the more obvious herbs and essences, while still keeping a tight lid on their family secrets.

The highlight is the bright, airy tasting area, so come with a full stomach and put it to the test – drink to your digestion, and toast the man who put the Lucano name on what is now an internationally-known brand.

Amaro Lucano's Museo Essenza Lucano is located at Pisticci Scalo, right off the SS407 Basentana highway.

More information: www.essenzalucano.it

13. Look for Invaders from the Tower in Tricarico

It's impossible to miss – the cylindrical tower makes itself seen. Which, of course, was the Normans' intention when they built it. Tricarico is not only beautifully endowed with monuments, it has the unusual distinction of being billed as *la citta' araba-normanna*. While the archeological finds show the area was a Lucani settlement, and the Lombards built a tower here in 849, they were fairly quickly chased off by the arrival of the Saracens, who built on the side of the hill. The old Arab districts are still there to wander, built in two parts, la Rabata and la Saracena. An ancient gateway still stands, as does a slender, graceful tower that looks out at cultivated fields. Above it, the web of alleys, some just slivers, is now a ghost town but fascinating to meander around. Below the district, the Arabs built terraced gardens, which are still used.

The Normans thundered in to Tricarico in 1048 and built uphill at the southern point, erecting the solid tower and turning their walled fortifications into a military command post. But they left the Saracen quarter intact. Maybe they figured it was better to keep those Saracens where they could see them.

And see them they could, for the rotund tower rises 88.5 feet, and, to make sure nothing was going to touch them, the walls were built 16 feet thick. They weren't playing around. It is also crowned with a rim for good measure. From the top, they surveyed the entire territory – down towards the Ionian Sea, north towards Melfi, and west towards the mountains. The best part is you can climb the tower and see what they were looking at.

It was built with four stories and the roof terrace really does offer breathtaking views. There is an intriguing anomaly, too. Standing on the disc in the center, you'll hear your own voice come back to you like in a cave. The tower was put on the National Monuments list in 1931, and is designated as a *patrimonio culturale* (cultural heritage site) by the region of Basilicata.

The strategic position made this an important city for the Normans, and the subsequent lords, so do take some time to look around. You'll be surprised by how many beautiful things are packed in here. The imposing Ducal Palace, convents decorated with frescoes, and palazzi all around town aren't what most people expect in a practically unknown town. The Romanesque **cathedral** is maybe most surprising, built in 1061 at the behest of Roberto Guiscardo, a Norman warrior knight. It was renovated in different styles in later years, but is lovely, and bears a big piece of history of its own: in 1383, Luigi I d'Angio was coronated king of Naples here.

From the lower Arab district to the dizzying height of the tower, Tricarico lets you look at the invaders from different perspectives.

Set up a tour to climb the tower through Zirlio (www.zirlio.it); they offer several different walking tours, as well.

14. Find the Lost Utopia at Campomaggiore Vecchio

NB: Campomaggiore is actually located in the Potenza Province, but it's great to combine it with your visit to Tricarico (#13) so I'm placing it here; it just "fits" the geography and logical itinerary better.

What is it about abandoned places that so captures our imaginations? Like Craco, the hamlet of Campomaggiore Vecchio was once a flourishing town with a pretty street plan and high ideals. It was so perfect, in fact, that it was dubbed "the city of Utopia".

There had been a Roman military outpost here called Campus Maiorem, that was abandoned. It was inhabited for a time in the Middle Ages, but sacked by Saracens and so the inhabitants fled to other towns. Under the Kingdom of Naples, the land holding was bestowed to the noble family Rendina in 1673, and a handful of families resided there.

After Count Teodoro Rendina took a Grand Tour of Europe, he came home inspired, and decided to create a notable town out of the hamlet that belonged to his family. He started enacting his ambitious dream of creating a utopia, a place of beauty where no poverty exists, bringing in architect Giovanni Patturelli, who was a student of Vanvitelli, in 1741. To repopulate Campomaggiore he decided that each farmer and tradesman would be given a house and a piece of land from which each family could grow what they needed. The allotments included some woodlands so each family would have wood for heating and cooking, but for each tree felled the family would have to plant three more.

A well-planned stone town was built, and included a church and the Rendina family *palazzo*, broad streets and a pair of piazzas for public gatherings. The Count's dream came true and the town did well; it grew from a population of 80 at the start of his experiment to 1,524 in 1885. That's the last census, because in that fateful year a massive landslide tumbled the utopian dream. There were no victims, except Campomaggiore itself. The residents fled to the country estate of the Rendina family on the hill a couple kilometers away, but the town was found to be uninhabitable again. It was later discovered that the substrata of the area was marshy and the water below the foundations shifted everything.

Come and take in the enormous views of the solitary location. Wander the ruins of the once-ideal town and see the majestic remains of the Palazzo Baronale, the family seat of the

Rendina, and the unmistakable bell tower, along with the ruined walls of the church itself. The Piazza dei Voti is now a field, so-named because it is where the first 16 families gathered with the Count to choose their allotments, and throw in their lots with the groundbreaking plan. Outlines of tumbling walls that were their houses and workshops are still visible. Stone sculptures by international artists are placed among the ruins, lending life to the ghost town.

If you're lucky to be here in August, you can see the spectral town come back to life, like a Brigadoon, in a magical show of theater, acrobatics and special effects, called (of course) La Citta' dell'Utopia. Combining mythical fantasy and history, it is a beautiful production. (Dates vary each year, so do check online if you're traveling in August.)

On the hill above sits the remains of the Rendina family summer residence, the Casino della Contessa, also worth a wander. The adjacent wine cellars and olive mill are still discernable. And speaking of olive mills, one of the best in Basilicata is located in Campomaggiore, the "new" town.

Be sure to take photos of Campomaggiore Vecchio to remind yourself that the ghostly town wasn't an apparition and that, at least for a little while, there was a real Utopia.

While You're Here...

Stop by the Di Perna *oleificio* for their excellent quality *olio extra-vergine*, even more delightful in the prettily painted ceramic bottles.

There's one more attraction here: the Ponte della Vecchia. Back down at the SS 407 highway is the medieval bridge that still stands over the Basento River, below the modern roadway. It is located just beyond the indoor swimming pool. There are signs. Park and walk down the dirt path on your left and you'll reach the gracefully arched stone span. Built in the 1400s, and restored in 1807, but local legend vehemently holds that the bridge was built by the Romans and that Hannibal and his troops crossed it on their Lucanian campaign. The rumble of the traffic on the highway overhead isn't so utopian, but the bridge is really lovely when seen from the riverbank on the opposite side.

More information:
https://www.campomaggiorecittadellutopia.it

15. Go Coast To Coast

There was a surprise hit movie a few years back called Basilicata Coast to Coast. The funny film featured a music group who decided to drum up attention for an upcoming concert by walking from Maratea on the Mediterranean to Scanzano Jonico on the Ionian Sea –from "coast to coast". Along the way they encountered a range of characters, scenes and foods that not only highlighted the region, but brought them into some hysterical circumstances.

You, too, can go from one coast to the other; while you may want to walk the 82 miles if you're an enthusiast, I think a car is an easier option for most travelers. You can do it in a day, too. What could be more enticing that sunrise over the Ionian

Sea and arriving in time to toast the sunset over the Med? It's a fun way to connect your Matera portion to a few days at the stunning resort town of Maratea –or vice versa, of course.

If you haven't already visited the Greek temples and archeology museum at Metaponto (#7) you really should do so before leaving this side of Basilicata. Also, pack a picnic lunch and make sure you have a full gas tank.

A good spot to watch the sunrise is the Marina di Pisticci beach. The pine-backed beach is the perfect place to sit on the sand with nothing but the sounds of nature and water as the first rays come up over the sea. OK; maybe a coffee in hand, too.

From there, it's an easy hop to the SS 653 road (also called the Sinnica) that meanders across the region to Lauria, and from there you'll take the squigglier roads down to the rocky shore of the Mediterranean coast. Along the way, the scenery will look more like the southwestern U.S. with almost desert-like landscapes, scrub-dotted hills and canyons, with mountains looming in the distance.

You'll find plenty of places to distract you. For example? Valsinni with its fairytale castle that holds a dark history. The poet Isabella Morra, born to an aristocratic family, was murdered here by her dastardly brothers for an exchange of poetic letters with a Spanish nobleman who lived in nearby Nova Siri. (They also murdered the Spaniard and then had to flee to France for inflaming a crisis with Spain.)

Across the valley and up the high hill is Colobraro, a town that's famous throughout Basilicata as "the town whose name you don't utter." (#8)

After Valsinni you'll cross the lake of Monte Cotugno, the largest rammed-earth dam in Europe. You can detour to Senise, home to addictive *peperoni cruschi* (#23). Francavilla in Sinni sits within the Pollino National Park boundaries, indicating you'll be passing green-sloped mountains along the route. Stretch your legs in Latronico and maybe catch some artwork (#21). The restaurant Taverna dei Gesuiti serves some inspired dishes while still keeping the regional traditions intact. Or, soothe your aches in the Latronico hot springs (open from May through October).

The drive takes you through stunning scenery, even if you don't detour to any of the towns. From seaside plains to canyons to mountains and valleys, then down to the rocky seashore, you'll pass through vast tracts of undisturbed nature not dissimilar to parts of the American West -not what most people expect to see in Italy.

When you reach the A2 autostrada you'll bid farewell to the SS 653 and either wind down to Lauria and then on to Maratea, or the easiest route is actually to take the highway a short jaunt north to Lagonegro and pick up the SS 585, and follow that all the way down to Castrocucco. From there you skirt along the coast to Maratea. It may be longer mileage but saves you the torturous curves. Unless you like torturous curves. Your call.

Welcome to Maratea and the west coast of Basilicata! You can head straight for the *porto* where there are bars and restaurants for drinks and dining; or, for a nice sunset view, go to Fiumicello beach, where parking is easy and you can grab a prosecco or Spritz at Le Pergole, sit on the sand to see the splash of colors as the sun goes down beyond the water and toast your coast to coast day.

Cin-cin!

MARATEA

THE PEARL OF THE MEDITERRANEAN

Strung along the Gulf of Policastro for 30 kilometers, Maratea is a pearl necklace of classic coastal beauty. Its name derives from *mare* (sea) and *dea* (goddess), and it is indeed a goddess of the sea. Rocky landscapes plunge to a sapphire sea, with sweet wildflowers and salt air mingling to provide a fragrant perfume. Beaches, reefs, coves and caves, a welcoming town, and the cleanest water imaginable, Maratea has it all. The only thing it lacks is crowds. Maratea is, in a word, enchanting.

Sitting on the side of Monte San Biagio, the compact *centro storico* is above the water, suspended between sea and sky. It's overlooked by a gigantic statue of Christ, the Redentore, while the town itself surveys the sea and surrounding hills.

Maratea is a seaside marvel – a beautiful pastel-painted hill town with a marina village below at the water's edge. It has all the charm of the more famous coastal towns but is widely unknown, much less crowded and less expensive. The mountains fall right into the sea and coves of exotic black sand beaches dot the shore. You can hike in the hills, swim in the Mediterranean, or lounge in the piazza, whatever your whim. This town is serviced by the rail line (a rarity among many coastal towns!), and has been awarded the prestigious Bandiera Blu (blue flag) for water and beach quality for twenty-four years running.

Its history stretches back to the Paleolithic era, and it was a trading center during Greek and Roman times; a load of amphorae and anchors was found shipwrecked below the little island of Santo Janno, now held in the civic museum of the town hall. The reality of Saracen raids in the 8th century was a deciding factor in moving to the upper town away from marauders. They burst out of the walls by the 11th century so the new *borgo*, Maratea Inferiore, was established by some of the residents, cleverly hiding the town in the fold of the mountain for protection.

Often cited to be "like the Amalfi Coast was before mass tourism," Maratea is still a rather quiet beach destination, thanks mostly to a bit of difficulty in arriving here. Ferries sometimes run in summer (and sometimes not); roads are squiggly. But once you're here, it's a piece of seaside paradise with quiet beaches (or busy ones, if you prefer), great food, and a *piazza* reminiscent of Capri's Piazzetta. It oozes that laid-back, sun-splashed atmosphere of uncrowded resort flair that people crave (but then end up at the over-crowded coasts, instead).

While you can arrive by train, getting around without a car can be a challenge, and orienting to the various zones can be confusing. Maratea isn't a single town center but a collection of outlying hamlets -11 of them, in fact- covering the hillside and the seashore. Here is a quick run-down:

Maratea Inferiore is the main town center, the "lower" town that was established in the Middle Ages. This is what most people mean when they say "Maratea" –where the town hall, *piazzetta*, shops and wine bars are located.

Maratea Superiore is the upper ancient town, the original settlement that was founded in the 7th century BC and inhabited by a parade of various rulers and invaders (the Byzantine, Lombards, Arabs, Normans, Spanish) before finally being destroyed by Napoleon's troops in 1806. The basilica dedicated to San Biagio (St. Blaise) and the towering landmark statue, il Redentore, are up there.

Maratea Marina is the middle ground where the train station sits, along with a section of sea coast below but there is no boat marina here as the name might suggest.

Maratea Porto is the charming port and marina where fishing boats sidle up next to yachts, and where the best restaurants are found, along with a marina *piazza* of umbrella-decked bars.

Acquafredda is a *frazione* to the north along the water, with coves and sea grottoes, some nice hotels, and a small hamlet, while **Cersuta** is another teensy village nearby. Both have some nice swimming coves, reachable by way of steps or by sea, so they're usually less crowded than the wider, sandy beaches closer to Maratea.

Maratea is called "the city of 44 churches" but because of all the outlying villages, the churches are scattered about, rather than all being concentrated in the old town center, as most people imagine. That doesn't mean there isn't a wealth of them there to visit, because you'll find several.

Now that you have the lay of the land (and sea), let's dive in to this pearl necklace adorning the sea goddess.

More information: www.visitmaratea.it (Italian only)

16. Make A Splash In Maratea

The stunning water beckons, and with 30 miles of coast in its realm, Maratea offers just the type of beach experience you crave, whether it be soft sand, a quiet cove, a rocky reef, or a hidden seawater "swimming pool." Because things are spread out and many beaches aren't marked, it can be a bit confusing to figure out where to go. Let me help you discover the best beaches of this marvelous seacoast. Splish-splash.

Black Sand. One of the hallmarks of Maratea's shore is the exotic-feeling black sand beaches. The color of the teensy dark pebbles seems to highlight the water all the more. Beware: the black color absorbs the heat and is nearly impossible to walk on without water shoes. I'd avoid these beaches in July and August unless it's a cloudy day!

Look for ***Lido Spiaggia Nera*** and ***Lido Cala Jannita*** off the SS 18 south of the port for the black sand beaches. You'll find sections of free beach (bring your own umbrella and beach blanket!) and *lido* concessions that rent sun beds and umbrellas. There are snack bars for beverages and lunch.

Long, Wide Sandy Beach. Many prefer an easily-accessible stretch of sand, and Maratea serves that up with style.

Fiumicello Beach. User-friendly, plenty of parking, and a long expanse of sand makes this beach popular, especially with families. No fuss, no hassle – just sun and splashing, along with restaurants, umbrellas and chair rentals (if you want them), and great sunsets.

Castrocucco. The biggest beach in the Maratea territory is found at the far southern part of the town's domain- right at the Calabria border, in fact. If you take a long stroll along the beach, you'll cross over into that region. (Woo hoo! Michelle Fabio fills you in on Calabria in her excellent book, *52 Things to See and Do in Calabria.*) The Castrocucco, also known as A'Gnola, beach is user-friendly, easy to park and plunk yourself on the sand, and the water deepens gradually, making it ideal for children.

Quiet Coves. There are some easily accessible coves, and others that require a bit of effort in the way of stairs or a path to reach, but worthwhile if you like to be in a cozy setting surrounded by the cliff rather than on a wide stretch of sand.

Cala Tunnara is near the port and popular with locals. Not many tourists find their way here. There are pieces of sand at low tide, otherwise you'll be on the rocks. Also called Mare Morto (dead sea) because it is protected, though the true "*mare morto*" part is a natural seawater swimming pool in the former fishing boat area, where the water is shallow and contained. Sea water splashes in to keep it clean and fresh.

Grotta della Scala. A dark pebble beach enclosed among the rocky cliffs, there is a managed beach with umbrellas and little sections and coves off to the sides that are free. You'll need to walk down more than 200 steps to reach it. It's near Villa Nitti; look for the Sombrero bar, who also manages the beach below. The path is next to the bar.

Porticello. A natural cove backed by Mediterranean *macchia* brush, a paved path brings you down to a little piece of paradise. A portion is set aside for Hotel Villa Cheta and Hotel San Diego above, while the rest is free. Behind it is the *Grotta del Dragone* –dragon's cave. Go inside…*if you dare!* You'll easily find the path next to the hotel.

Day-use "Destination Beaches". These lovely spaces are called parks and you'll see why – the umbrellas are tucked in among rocks and plants, with secluded corners, grassy sun areas, and good dining available. They're really a full-day destination rather than a quick splash kind of beach. You pay for parking and pay an entrance fee, but you get a very nice experience for it. You can bring your own snacks and drinks, if you'd like.

La Secca and ***Il Mirto Solarium.*** Honestly? This is my favorite. I love how it's laid out to give you space, and I like the more natural feel and deeper water at **Il Mirto.** We're swimmers, so shallow water bores us. Here we can snorkel and swim over to the opposite "island" rocks. At next-door **La Secca,** there are kayaks and pedal boats for rent to scoot around the area. The two parks are next to each other, owned by brothers, separated by an old monastic building. As you drive in, you decide which one you want where the road branches off. Even the parking is nice – under trees and arbors. Both establishments have a lovely atmosphere, though if you prefer a beachy section to enter the water rather than a ladder, you'll want La Secca, with umbrellas on the half-shell beach and scattered above. They are located south of the Marina di Maratea zone.

Illicini. Another *parco* with two cove beaches of black pebbles set amidst the jagged rocks, with umbrellas and sun beds tucked in among the *mirto* and juniper brush. One beach area looks at the little island of Santo Janni and is practically enclosed by rocks, creating a lagoon-like pool. Very nice!

Only by Sea Beaches. Want to really enjoy a day away from everything? Then check out the beaches that are accessible only by way of the sea. Rent a boat or kayak (#19) and visit these natural gems, without lines of umbrellas, snack bars, or crowds.

Funnicu Reggiu. Also called ***Filocaio***, this *piccolo paradiso* can be reached easily by kayak or rented boat, and is worth the effort because it is gah-geous! It's a short distance south of the port, but no trails arrive here; you can reach it only by sea. A big rock stands at the beach, there's space to sun, and there's shade closer to the rock wall. Gloriously clear water, and few people. This is one of our favorite spots to kayak to.

L' Vranne. This one attracts more folks now, after having been named the most beautiful beach in Italy a couple of years ago. Before that, nobody knew about it except the locals. But never mind, because even with its new-found status, it still isn't packed with people. You can arrive by rental boat or swim over from the black sand beach, though that has a distinct drawback – there are no services here, so if you swim, you won't be able to take towels or bottled water along. Another option? Rent a pedal boat at the *spiaggia nera*!

17. Go To Rio (Sort Of), And Walk In The Footsteps Of A Saint

Without a doubt, the defining feature of Maratea is the towering statue of Christ up on the pinnacle high above the sea. It is, of course, reminiscent of the taller one above Rio de Janeiro. But, as they point out around here, Rio's is set on a tall base that ups its height, like platform shoes. Installed in 1965, Il Redentore has his arms outstretched towards the land (embracing the people) with his back to the sea. Do I even have to mention the massive views you'll get up there?

The road to reach the lofty site is itself a feat of engineering with its cantilevered curves. It's panoramic, but who can peel their eyes off the suspended roadway to look? The arrival at Maratea Superiore will have you heaving a sigh of relief, and you may even want to duck inside the Basilica of San Biagio to say a prayer of thanks at surviving the hair-raising road. Even if your courage didn't waver, you'll want to visit the basilica, because out of Maratea's 44 churches, this is the one considered most important, as far as the *Marateoti* are concerned. You see, San Biagio (St. Blaise) is the city's patron saint.

The church isn't particularly adorned; in fact, inside you'll find the 15th century fresco of the Madonna, some scattered marble bas relief sculptures, and the heavy silver statue of the saint – and not much else in the way of artwork. But the site is revered and the saint is said to have arrived here miraculously – found in a shipwreck on the tiny island of Santo Janni below, and the people set about busily to build the church to house his remains. In another legend, they say the basilica was built over an ancient pagan temple dedicated to the goddess Minerva, thus putting the *dea* in the Mare-dea name. No actual archeological evidence has been found, but it makes for a better story, dontcha think?

The "dispute" of San Biagio. If you visit in May, you'll be able to enjoy the city's four-day *festa* in honor of their patron saint, with a bit of southern Italian drama. It takes place during the second week of May, the most dramatic part being the Thursday procession to carry the saint's statue along the mountain path from its year-round residence down to Maratea town, that has had a long-held dispute over the festivities of St. Blaise. For the procession, the saint is swathed in a red drape covering to represent his neutrality in the feud. Upon his arrival at Capo Casale above the *centro storico*, the statue is uncovered, San Biagio is given the keys to the city by the mayor. And a party ensues. He stays in town until Sunday, when he is carried back to his mountaintop home.

But back to that lofty landmark. From here you can see three Italian regions in one sweep of the head – from Campania to the north, the Basilicata coast, and on down to Calabria. The folds of the landscape, the incredible deep color of the water and green mountains behind, the clouds skidding by, and Christ right there with you – you'll think you're in heaven.

Below the statue is the original hamlet of Maratea Superiore, now a ghost town, but fascinating and beautiful in its disrepair. Take a stroll along the cobbled streets amidst the crumbling stone homes. A path connects it to Maratea Inferiore below, so walkers can enjoy a panoramic hike rather than driving. If you don't have a car, there are buses from the various sections of Maratea to reach Castello/Redentore.

18. Marvel at the Grotta delle Meraviglie

It's easy to whiz by the sign pointing to the Grotta della Meraviglia, or Cave of Marvels, but you should go looking for it because the underground wonders really will amaze you.

It was discovered by chance when road workers were putting in the SS 18 in the 1920s. A fallen hammer slipped into the void and the astounded worker found not only his hammer but a magical underworld, as well.

Driving the coastal road, the Grotta is found in the area called Marina di Maratea. There is a small parking area along the SS 18, roughly across the street from the entrance. Walking down a set of stairs to the door, you cross the threshold to earthly depths where minerals and water have created a sculptural fantasyland. It is a natural work of art formed over the span of several millennia. There are stalactite cascades and strands of mineral-dripping spaghetti; columns and glistening diamonds, all right below the road. It culminates at the stalagmite Nativity scene, something special to behold.

The compact cavern is the smallest in Italy, measuring in at just 90 meters long (about a half-mile) with a descent of only eight meters, but it packs a whopping visual punch that will leave you marveling during the 30-minute journey of wonders. Even my geologist hubby was duly impressed.

Be sure to bring a jacket; despite its short span and shallow depth it's a bit chilly inside, even in summer.

There are set, regular visiting hours during high season (June through September) and the guides are also proficient in English. If you want to make sure, call in advance to request an English-language guide. In other seasons, the Grotta is open by appointment. If you have a group, you can request a private tour (but be sure to set it up in advance).

Love geology and want to continue on a cavern theme? Visit some of the sea caves along the coast, by boat or by kayak (#19).

The Grotta delle Meraviglie is located on SS 18, 200 meters (650 feet) south of the turn-off for the Spiaggia Nera (black sand beach, #16). There is parking along the side road, 80 meters north of the cavern's sign and entrance.

Grotta delle Meraviglie – Cavern of Marvels –
www.mondomaratea.it (Italian);
www.maratea.info (also in English)
Phone: (+39) 895 895 5586

19. Row, Row, Row Your Boat

(Or Cheat With A Motor)

The beauty of this spectacular coastline is best seen by sea, and for that you have to get out on the water. A kayak gives you the perfect way to get away from the land, explore the coves and magically-lit sea caves, and view the rocky formations along the shore.

Fly Maratea may seem a strange name for kayak outings and rentals, but make no mistake, that's what they offer down at the *porto*. Their half-day guided paddles will take you to things you'd miss on your own, like caves that refract light and cast blue and green shades (like the super-famous Blue Grotto in Capri, but without anyone else around). We enjoyed the hidden beaches where we could sun and splash in blissful solitude. The guide pointed out formations and history and gave us a fun, if tiring, tour. Going it on your own lets you set the pace, but you'll have to keep your eyes open and be willing to explore a bit to find the seaborne gems.

If you don't know how to paddle, they'll give you a quick lesson before setting off.

If that all sounds like too much work, there are a few boat tours that do the motoring for you while giving you fab views and the chance to dive in to that enticingly blue water along the way. Choose the southern route or northern one – you can't really go wrong as there are joys along both. (Or do both!)

Heading north, our expert skipper, Andrea, showed us special spots and anchored so we could swim into a cave that first sparkled like it was scattered with diamonds, and then shimmered in an other-worldly blue. There are romantic sunset cruises, too, for the epic color-splatters that happen when the sun goes down beyond the sea, accompanied by glasses of bubbly and local cheese and other nibbles. The return to the port is heart-warming, coming in by water like so many arrived here for centuries before the modern roads were built.

If you're spending some time here, I recommend taking at least one of the boat tours to get a lay of things from the sea; then if you're up for it, rent a boat for a half-day so you can return to that little quiet cove, or that sandy beach reached only by the water. Pack a picnic, get away (even though there aren't many crowds here to flee from) and have a seafaring experience all your own.

More Information:

Fly Maratea – For kayak rentals and guided excursions www.fly-maratea.it

Boat Excursions – Nautilus Escursioni, 3.5 hours morning or afternoon; sunset excursions on request. Contact Andrea by email at nautilusescursioni@gmail.com. Or visit his Facebook page.

Marvin Escursioni – Captain Giovanni takes you on similar half-day outings. Find him on Facebook.

Rentals – Rent a boat from the port through La Rosa dei Venti; email: chico.25@hotmail.it

Or, line up the rentals and excursions on site when you arrive.

20. Explore Your Wild Side in the Pollino National Park

If you're into snow-dusted peaks, mountain's majesty and alpine valleys, then you'll revel in the Pollino National Park, which just happens to be Italy's largest. It unfolds between Basilicata and Calabria, with 182,012 hectares –that's 702 square miles, 342 of which are in Basilicata. The vast wilds include 24 towns within the park's borders, that cling tightly to their deep traditions. Two of them, San Paolo Albanese and San Costantino Albanese, are Albanian towns and well worth visiting.

But what you really need to know about the Pollino is summed up in one word: Spectacular. The rugged, raw beauty is primeval and breathtaking. It basically has everything you'd expect from a national park: loads of trails, stunning views, glacial formations, alpine lakes, deep forests, rocky mountains. In fact, now that I think of it, this part of the region does remind me of Colorado. Be on the look-out for the park's fauna; you just might spot the rare dormouse that makes its home here, along with a native species of roe deer, wild horses, Peregrine falcons, golden eagles and several species of owls.

There are plenty of ways to go wild here, with adventures for every level. No matter what you prefer, though, there is one caveat: you must (MUST!) see the Bosnian pine trees that are the symbol of the park. These massive, sculpted beasts are hundreds of years old, found exclusively here and the Balkans. You can see them throughout the park, but the best place is the Giardino degli Dei, the garden of the gods, an alpine valley filled with them. One, called the Patriarch, is believed to be nearly 1,000 years old. The best way to find the *pino loricato* and to explore the park is with a guide.

The Pollino is very expansive and there are several gateways. They are all lovely towns – Rotonda, Viggianello, San Severino Lucano or Terranova di Pollino, any of which make a great base. For what it's worth, Viggianello is classified among the prettiest towns in Italy *(i borghi piu' belli d'Italia)*, and for those who like adventure in the great outdoors but not in lodgings, you will appreciate the Castello dei Principi hotel that lets you sleep in a castle. Rotonda is where the Eco-Museo visitor's center is located, an environmental-educational center with interactive displays set in a former monastery. Terranova has the advantage of being near two of the Albania villages (#42), and the region's most acclaimed restaurant (See Dining Experiences in the back of the book).

Real hiking enthusiasts can take advantage of the many

rifugi, mountain hostels that usually have great food, too. There are many, along with lots of scattered *agriturismi* farm stays throughout the area. If you like to bag peaks, you can hit five of them; while the highest peak Monte Dolcedormire (7,437 feet above sea level) is across the border in Calabria, the second is only slightly lower –Monte Pollino is 7,375 feet up in the clouds.

There's so much more than trekking going on here, though. Winter brings snow-shoeing and Nordic skiing, while summer lets you float down a river on a tube or run the rapids on a raft. An unusual thing is *acqua trekking* – river walking, in either low-flow streams or high-energy torrents with cascades that you shimmy down; it's something memorable! Rock climbing, hang gliding, horse riding. One tour guide (Info Pollino) takes you foraging for chestnuts and wild mushrooms, so there are plenty of ways to go wild. No matter how you define that.

Pollino National Park website: www.parcopollino.gov.it (Also in English) A list of hiking and climbing guides can be found here.

Pollino River Tubing – Is there anything as fun as tubing? Find their Facebook page

Pollino Acqua Trekking gives you waders and takes you into the river. www.pollinoacquatrekking.com

Info Pollino is a group of guides that organizes excellent adventures including tubing, trekking, foraging and more, for all levels. www.infopollino.com

21. Indulge in Modern Art in the Great Outdoors in the Pollino National Park

The Pollino National Park is best known for its immense pristine mountain landscapes where the twisted trunks of the *pino loricato* trees are truly natural sculptures and where the intense turquoise skies with cotton-candy clouds are like paintings. But there's also a contemporary art project that adds a cultural aspect and some whimsy to the great outdoors –Arte Pollino.

The project was promoted by the region, the Ministry of Cultural Heritage, and the Biennale of Venice. With a motto that it is "*lo spazio naturale dell'arte*" –the natural place for art, the goal is to take inspiration in nature and combine it with large-scale installations. As one of the artists, Anna Rapinoja, said, the art is "a mediator of nature's messages."

The headquarters is in the hot springs town of Latronico (soak away the aches from all that hiking!) where the installation Earth Cinema is found, by internationally known artist Anish Kapoor. "It is where you can hear the echo of Mother Earth," he says.

Near Noepoli is the Teatro Vegetale –an arc-shape using plants and rocks to delineate the natural theater formed by the landscape itself.

At San Paolo Albanese, the artist took elements of the town's history and the importance of Spanish broom, which was used to make actual brooms, of course, but was also used for fabrics and threads. Sky Cleaner comprises giant upended brooms planted in the earth that move slightly in the breeze and "clean the sky of grey clouds".

The most whimsical piece is an interactive one, too. It's found near San Severino Lucano, where Carsten Holler, who has works in the Tate Modern, installed R-B Ride, a sort of uplifted merry-go-round, and yes, you can actually ride it. The moving (literally) artwork is placed at a panoramic point and slowly (very, very slowly) makes a rotation in an up-tilted position. The artist deliberately set the ride with its twelve colorful cars at a snail's pace –it takes fifteen minutes for a once-around- to give spectators the chance to observe nature in a deliberate way and from several different perspectives at once.

In Basilicata's Pollino National Park, you can enjoy nature's art as well as art *in* nature –it's a win-win, no?

More Information: www.artepollino.it (Also in English)

22. Attend a Weird Wedding

Southern Italian weddings are blow-out parties with hours of feasting, drinking and merry dancing that make My Big Fat Greek Wedding look mild. But there are some, uh let's say unusual, weddings that take place here that...well, you have to see them to understand.

The marriage of the trees is an ancient pagan rite that many towns in Basilicata still observe, one might say, religiously. The sacred and profane come together in mysterious and mystical ceremonies that harken back to the ancient Lucani people. It's just that now they are also tied (one might say "married") to a religious feast day, as well.

The so-called *riti arborei* are still practiced in nine towns around the region, and while there are several names for the *festa*, each celebration is an almost primeval joining of man and nature, with a dash of fertility ritual (sort of like the ancient equivalent of the *nonnas* at modern Italian weddings nudging the newlyweds to "get started" on a family). In my area of central Basilicata in the Dolomiti Lucane mountains, they are called "il Maggio" but despite what might imply May in the name, they generally take place in June. The most famous is in tucked-away Accettura.

So just what's the wedding? Two trees are selected – usually a towering beech or mighty oak, the "Maggio," which represents the groom; and a fir or holly tree top, the "*Cima*," the bride. To say they take the selection and cutting of the trees seriously is an understatement. They obsessively comb the mountains for just the right *alberi* for this arranged marriage. On the designated day, they are felled and transported separately (groom can't see the bride before the wedding!) in two processions, either carried on the shoulders of a team of worthy men, or by oxen. The trees are then joined in mystic matrimony and raised up as a towering totem. Then the wedding is "consummated" when courageous (or crazy) youths climb to the top.

As with all good weddings, there is singing, dancing and dining in the presence of the bridal couple. Sometimes prayers for a good harvest are part of the ritual (that fertility thing).

There are a few differences among the nine towns; for instance, Terranova di Pollino is the only town that raises one single, carefully selected fir tree rather than grafting two together. Most are held to coincide with the feast of St. Anthony of Padova (but not all).

If you want to attend one of the weddings, here is the rundown of where and when they take place (no gift registries needed):

Central Basilicata
(Dolomiti Lucane mountains)

Accettura –Il Maggio di Accettura, a four-day festival in June, the Sunday after Pentecost.

Pietrapertosa – Il Mascio, takes place in June over the feast day of Sant'Antonio (June 13).

Castelmezzano – La Sagra du Masc', is held in September even though it also celebrates St. Anthony.

Oliveto Lucano – Il Maggio, held the third Sunday of August.

Gorgoglione – Il Maggio, held on June 12 at the Santuario della Madonna, and the tree meets the Madonna in a procession.

Southern Basilicata
(Pollino National Park)

Viggianello – L'a' Pitu e la Rocca, last week of August to celebrate St. Francis of Paola, the town's patron saint.

Terranova di Pollino – A'Pit (derives from *l'abete*, or spruce), held in June the week leading up to St. Anthony's day (June 13) culminating in the wedding on the feast day.

Rotonda – La Pitu e la Rocca (the groom is the *pitu*, the bride is the *rocca*), the week leading up to June 13, the wedding day.

Castelsaraceno – La 'Ndenna e la Cunocchia, June 12-19 (the joining and raising of the trees is June 19).

For more information see www.ritiarboreilucani.it (Italian) or www.basilicataturistica.it/en/riti-arborei (English).

23. BITE INTO THE S-CRUNCH-OUS PEPERONI CRUSCHI IN SENISE

If there is a single signature food that defines Basilicata, this is it. It came as a surprise to us that the strings of red peppers drying in the southern sun aren't fiery like we'd thought. They sure resembled the chile ristras we were used to seeing around New Mexico. While southerners do like the spice of the *piccante* variety, those are distinctly smaller and not as highly revered as these babies. The longer red peppers are, in fact, a variety of sweet peppers and you'll find them only here in Basilicata.

The peppers are called *peperone di Senise*, and they have IGP designation, which means they're a geographical-specific product grown around the towns of Senise, Noepoli, Chiaromonte, and on down the Sinni river valley to Montalbano Jonico. Like most things around here, the seemingly simple pepper has a long history. They were brought to Europe by the Spanish when they returned from the Caribbean –specifically from the Antilles- then made the jump from Spain to Italy under the Aragon rule of the Kingdom of Naples. How the varietal ended up in this valley is left to the imagination, but the plant found favorable growing conditions in the alluvial lime-sand soil and abundant sunshine, so here we are. Centuries later and these garnet-red sweet peppers are truly a thing.

Mostly, they are dried and then used in ingenious ways. If they're eaten fresh, it is usually in a *peperonata* where they are fried with onions, garlic and tomato, a real burst of summer in that dish. But as I said, the majority of them are dried and that's when the magic happens. They are turned into *peperoni cruschi* (KROO-skee), a sort of harsh-sounding dialect word that aptly describes the crunch of them when the dried peppers are flash-fried in olive oil. The salted crispy peppers shatter in your mouth in a burst of flavor, and like potato chips, I bet you can't eat just one. No, you'll want the whole plate! They are addictive.

But the joy of *peperoni cruschi* doesn't stop at the snack or *antipasto* level. Once fried, they are used in a bunch of different dishes. Most notably and cleverly, the peasant usage was to crumble them over pasta dishes as an extra flavoring in lieu of grated cheese. Cheese was often eaten fresh as a protein source and the subsistence farmers didn't have the luxury of setting aside cheese to age for grating. But out of those poor roots came big flavors, and so they devised an excellent solution by seasoning crumbled breadcrumbs and frying them in some olive oil, then crumbling in some of the *peperoni cruschi*, too. This mixture was then sprinkled over pasta dishes, like the region's famous *cavatelli con la mollica di pane* that you encounter all over Basilicata. They are also frequently crushed over *orecchiette* (little ears pasta) with *cima di rape* (rapini) greens. And on pork or lamb dishes. And…well, visit one of the restaurants around Senise to see, and you'll quickly understand why they're called "*l'oro rosso lucano*" – the red gold of Lucania.

The dried peperoni are also ground (without frying) and the powder is used in the region's famous sausages (#31) and salami.

By the by, while they are most commonly called *peperoni cruschi* around most of the region, here in the Senise area they have a different dialect word–*zafaran*'. Go figure.

And, one more piece of trivia – emigrants from this area took the seeds with them to America, and many descendants report memories of *cruschi* being made by their grandmothers. They were so common in the Italian-American community in Chicago that they were called "Melrose peppers".

While you're here, it is absolutely obligatory to try them. I know one taste is all it will take for you to call them "s-crunchous" and look for ways to stuff your suitcase with them.

24. Revel in the Little Pompeii of Basilicata

That adage "all roads lead to Rome" wasn't wrong. Those famous arteries linked the capital to the far-flung reaches of the empire, and the super-highway Appian Way came down to the south, then branched off. Here in Basilicata, the Roman city of Grumentum grew along the crossroads of the Via Popilia that went to Reggio Calabria, and the Via Herculea that went over to Heraclea (now Policoro). This was no backwater town. The city was so important it had the only Roman amphitheater in Lucania.

Grumentum claimed some ancient stars, too: Spartacus passed through here with his rebel forces. And before that, Hannibal encamped here and won the support of the populace for the Carthaginian cause (or, at least, turned them against the Romans). Unfortunately for the Carthaginians, the Romans routed Hannibal's forces in 207 BC and he was forced to flee by way of Spinoso, and up towards Laurenzana and Anzi (then Anxia). The locals paid a heavy penance for the sin of siding against Rome. Hannibal, who was known for his courage, intelligence and tenacity as well as his pack elephants, lost 8,000 men, and maybe one of the pachyderms; remains of one were found near Rotonda. Who knows if it wasn't a fallen war animal from one of his battles?

All this history is steeped into the streets and ruins at Grumentum, which is called "*la piccola Pompeii di Basilicata.*" The city's evidence is abundant and impressive –and (even better) uncrowded. On our visits we've never encountered more than five other folks wandering around, giving us plenty of space and silence to contemplate the place. On two visits, there were sheep amidst the ruins, their bells providing a melody to our historical musings. Start at the Archeology Museum (the Museo Archeologico Nazionale Dell'Alta Val D'Agri) for an overview and in-depth look at the artifacts.

Walk along the stone Roman road where ruts from the chariots' iron wheels are still visible. Then dig into the ruins, where the amphitheater outline is clearly discernible; there is a pair of temples, plus the forum and houses, all built with the distinctive Roman diamond-pattern of stones. The mosaics blew me away, so don't miss them, especially the House of Mosaics. But the bath complex is one of the most intriguing spots, as you can see how the water was heated and carried to the rooms and it is considered one of the best preserved in the world. This is where the most imaginative mosaic was uncovered: it depicts marine creatures. Then there is the theater, where shows took place, as opposed to gladiator games in the amphitheater. If you come in the summer, you can take in a show or concert here, too, which is a really amazing experience (understatement!)

Ancient Grumentum declined after the Roman Empire collapsed, finally giving up and moving uphill after some Saracen sackings rattled their nerves. Some residents fled to Marsicovetere and Viaggiano (#25). Go on up to Grumento Nova to see the medieval town that followed in the wake of the once-glorious city in the valley.

There's really no reason to *not* go to Grumentum: not only is it a fascinating and impressive place where you can have the luxury of exploring without crowds or tacky souvenir sellers; it costs a mere €2.50 to explore. So, go and revel in the little Pompeii of Basilicata.

Information is shockingly lacking on this gem; see this site: https://www.cuorebasilicata.it/grumentum

25. Pay Homage to the Queen of Basilicata in Viggiano

She wears a crown and sits enthroned with her son, the Prince, in a palatial home built for her. Her name is Maria, but she is called La Regina della Basilicata, the queen, and is the region's preferred saint. She is most commonly referred to as *la madonna nera*, the black Madonna.

Hers is a story of beauty from ashes. The origins of the delicate wood-carved statue are uncertain; some say it was created in the 6th or 7th century, fitting with its Byzantine style. It is known to have been venerated in Grumentum (#24), and when that city was destroyed by Saracens, the inhabitants fled to Viggiano, Marsicovetere and Grumento Nova. The story holds that the clergy who left Grumentum came here and buried the statue on top of Monte di Viggiano, at 5,659 feet above sea level, for safe keeping. The local lore then says that a couple of centuries later some shepherds saw strange flashes of light like fire coming from the peak and discovered the icon, miraculously intact. They took it to town and it was placed in the chapel of Santa Maria Fuori le Mura. Not long after, they set about building the sanctuary on the mountain on the spot where the statue was discovered. Some records indicate a mountain chapel was built before 1393, though the current structure dates to the 1500s. The exposed hole next to the altar is where the Madonna Nera had been found, and the mountain became known as *il sacro monte*, or sacred mountain.

The devotion to the black Madonna never waned and faithful followers came from all over the area. She was clothed in a solid-gold gown during the Spanish period, and is, in fact, strikingly similar to the Madonna di Monserrat. In 1890 Pope Leo XIII declared her the protectoress saint of Basilicata. Helping her out is the region's patron saint, San Gerardo Maiella of

Muro Lucano (#32). Viggiano, for its part, is called *la citta' di Maria* (the city of Mary). It also bears another moniker, too (see #26).

Her home, the *chiesa madre* (mother church) has an elegant palace-like façade befitting of the queen. Those beautiful bronze doors, by the way, are the work of a Lucano sculptor, Marco Santoro, who carved the story of the sanctuary and the statue in six detailed scenes. Look for the local flora carved in there, too. The church holds some lovely paintings by regional artists, but of course, it's not the palace but the queen that garners the attention.

Every year two processions take place in her regal honor–on the first Sunday of May to carry the statue to the mountain chapel where it remains for the summer; and on the first Sunday of September, when she is carried back to the basilica in town. Lest you think this is any ordinary walk, you should realize it is an 11-kilometer trek. Uphill. The men have to do it while carrying a weighty gold-covered statue enclosed within an ornate wooden protective case. The processions are filled with ceremony and ritual, accompanied by *zampogne* (rustic bag pipes) and marching band music. On reaching the chapel, they encircle it three times before entering, and many of the pilgrims touch the Madonna's box with olive branches or flowers; thousands of devotees attend. The following day there is a party in the piazza that draws even more numbers.

Don't miss the life-sized sculpture that sits in Piazza Papa Giovanni XXIII, at the entrance to town. It would be hard to miss anyway; it's the second largest monument in the region, after Maratea's towering Redentore (#17). The Madonna e I Suoi Portatori depicts the treasured procession and the men who carry the Madonna in faithful devotion.

No matter when you visit, the queen of Basilicata is always there on her throne, ready to greet you and extend her regal benediction.

While You're Here…Viggiano is also known as the city of *petrolio*, so that industrial plant you can see from the overlook in front of the basilica is an oil-extraction facility. It is the largest oil reserve in Italy, garnering the Viggiano – Val d'Agri zone the title, "the Texas of Italy". An inspiring view it isn't, and it has brought wealth along with controversy and contamination. More inspiring? The uphill view from the top of the Monte Sacro, in the Parco dell'Appenino Lucano, where you're likely to see hawks and eagles dancing on the winds.

26. Strum a Song on a Harp in Viggiano

Alongside its title as *Città di Maria* (#25) and status as keeper of the queen, Viggiano has another title – *la città dell'arpa*, the city of the harp. Can you hear the airy chords as I recount the history?

Nobody knows exactly how this particular town took up music as a vocation, but for hundreds of years, Viggiano has been renowned for its performers of stringed instruments – lutes, violins, and especially, harps. There were many workshops in the 1700s that produced hand-made instruments, the most unique of which were small, lightweight, portable harps. Usually with fewer than 20 strings, they could be carried easily over the shoulder, and it was this *arpa viggianese* that gave Viggiano's musicians an edge.

They were itinerant players, traveling from town to town playing for religious feast days and devotional rites. The Viggianesi were especially well-received in Naples and as their fame spread, so did their opportunities. They generally formed small bands of three to four instruments, who found plenty of work as they moved around the country, and then around Europe. Often, it was a family unit, and they played for several months, then returned home and tended their farms. Music was a profitable supplement to their agricultural sustenance. Others took it as a full-time profession, considered more a *mestiere* (trade) than an art in those days.

In Viggiano census documents, they reported that one in three families listed a musician among their ranks; by the mid-1800s there were 300 Viggianese harpists performing around the world. They learned to play by ear at an early age, as most didn't read music. As Viggiano's musicians emigrated, so did the harps, and they were taken around the globe.

Made from pine, oak or cherry wood from the forests above Viggiano, each instrument was truly a work of craftsmanship, every piece unique. The music sort of faded away as the population did, and the workshops died off. That is, until a few years ago, when a local initiative took up the strains of musical pride and started once again creating the Viggiano harps in town. More than that, the city now has a music school dedicated to the harp, the only one in Italy, as well as a remote campus for the Conservatorio Gesualdo da Venosa music school.

While it's unlikely they'll let you strum the harps, you can see examples of them in the Villa del Marchese, which also hosts musical recitals; the Museo delle Tradizioni Locali also has some, along with items relating to by-gone rural life. There are operas, popular folk music, Jazz, and concerts highlighting only harps throughout the year, so do check to see if you might be able to attend one. The biggest is the annual Rassegna dell'Arpa Viggianese held every summer that brings in international musicians.

You can see the importance the instruments held here as you stroll around town; many a door portal has a harp or violin carved into the stone. Also, be sure to look for the harp player on the bronze doors of the basilica; at least you can pretend to strum the strings as you hum a Neapolitan folk song or a rural tarantella.

More information:
http://www.comune.viggiano.pz.it/turismo (Italian)

27. Eat to Your Heart in Sarconi

Remember that little ditty about beans, beans they're good for your heart? In Sarconi, they definitely sing the praises of their local legumes. Here, the humble bean is exalted for its health benefits, its versatility, as well as its agricultural and economic contribution to the area. The Fagioli di Sarconi even received special IGP status, giving them street cred.

Sarconi sits in the upper Agri River valley (the Val d'Agri), where the legumes, that were originally brought to Europe from the Americas in the 1500s, have optimal fertile conditions in the river-fed fields and mild summer climate that doesn't burn them out. The legal growing area isn't limited just to Sarconi; it extends through the upper Val d'Agri, so the beans are also grown in Grumento Nova, Tramutola, Marsico Nuovo, Moliterno and Spinoso.

But never mind the technicalities; it's the beans that count. The Fagioli di Sarconi isn't actually one varietal but a rainbow of beans – red, violet, black white, brown, greenish and bi-colored (I like the palomino-looking one myself). They are small and round and are rather *dolce* (sweet) when cooked. That alone makes them popular in many households, but they also have thin skins, which reduce the cooking time (most of them are dried rather than eaten fresh).

The varieties have some amusing names. There is the *tabacchino* (little tobacco) for its color, and the *ciuoti*, which makes me laugh because that's a southern word used for "foolish" or "daft". When I looked it up, there is some indication that the term was actually taken from the name of the bean, so when I hear someone on the street calling his friend a *ciuoto*, I smile. You bean!

Let's get down to the meat of the matter, though, because they really do know beans in Sarconi, especially delectable ways to cook them. They are rich in protein and mineral salts, and have been a staple in the area's diets for centuries. In winter, there's polenta with a nice saucy bean topping. Of course, there are many soups; beyond the classic *pasta e fagioli*, there is pumpkin and bean soup, and a mixed bean soup with pancetta. There is no end of ingenuity when mixing them with pasta –the Italian creativity can make those simple plates worthy of royalty! They are especially good when cooked in a clay pot in the fireplace; a good, long simmering, and then mixed with short pasta – heaven. Or, just cooked beans topped with that savory Lucanica sausage (#31), a wonderful one-pot meal.

(The Italian version of beany weenie?) Then there's the *baccalà* dish (#34) with *peperoni cruschi* (#23) and beans. And. In Sarconi, beans aren't limited to main dishes, oh no. Because they're *dolce*, they're also used to make some desserts. Really. Try it!

You can sample the whole gamut if you're here for the blowout Festa del Fagiolo on August 18 and 19. If not, you can sure eat to your heart in any of the restaurants around the area. Maybe just forget that the middle part of the children's ditty and skip to the "let's eat beans for every meal" part. Sarconi is built on a hill of beans and they're ready to spill them for you.

Where to dine? The logical place is Il Fagiolo d'Oro (the golden bean), an *agriturismo* that also provides some lovely overnight rooms. The restaurant and rooms are both strictly by reservation, though, so plan ahead.

While You're Here – You can't leave Sarconi without stopping at the **Acquedotto Cavour.** The 19th century rebuild of the previous Roman aqueduct carried water to Sarconi and Moliterno. It is right off the Via Cavour at the edge of town. It probably watered those Sarconi beans, don't you think? Park in Via Cavour and walk the length of the arched structure.

More information: http://www.fagiolidisarconi.it

28. Go to the Moon (and back) in Sasso di Castalda

Sasso di Castalda was a sleepy hamlet hidden on the green slopes of Monte Arioso, southwest of Potenza, the classic stone buildings and alleyways seemingly stuck in time from centuries past. Until, that is, they reached for the moon. They decided to honor one of their hometown heroes in a big way – with a 984-foot long Tibetan bridge called the *Ponte alla Luna*, or bridge to the moon. Rocco Petrone, the director of launch operations at Cape Kennedy Space Center and Apollo program director for NASA may have been born in America, but his parents were both *Sassesi*, thus, the town's pride has always swelled for this renowned rocket scientist.

Sasso di Castalda heralds Rocco Petrone, but the focus is on the bridge – which may well seem like walking to the moon.

It is suspended over a deep void 335 feet above the ground. Gulp. To reach the opposite side you need to place your feet on 770 steps, one at a time, with enough space between them to be just a tad unnerving, while also tending to your safety harness and clips along the way. There is a "baby bridge" first that will test your stamina and resolve for the longer, higher moon walk; you can chicken-out here and head back to the cafes of town to console yourself. Or, you can take that proverbial "one giant step" and plunge forward.

The smaller bridge leaves from the old town and crosses the gorge. From there, you walk the trail that skirts the rock and leads up to the launch pad. Once on the Ponte alla Luna, you'll feel like you're walking through space to reach the ruins of a castle on a rocky outcropping high over the gulley. Naturally, a selfie is in order to prove your courage, and don't overlook the breathtaking views that surround you (if you can peel your eyes off those footholds!) Once you reach the "moon", an earth-bound trail takes you back through the pretty streets of Sasso di Castalda.

Don't have the daring? That's okay; you can enjoy the panoramic terrace called the Skywalk – a glass platform cantilevered over the stunning landscape. And there are plenty of forest paths for traditional hiking. Hard-core *vie ferrate* climbing routes are for those who find the Ponte alla Luna too wimpy. An energetic group of locals also offers E-Bike tours in the Parco Nazionale dell'Appenino Lucano (the national park of which Sasso is a part). In short, there's plenty for outdoors lovers to enjoy, plus some restaurants for a good post-lunar voyage meal. Stroll around the timeless *centro storico* to bring you back to earth -and Basilicata's old-world charm.

Ponte alla Luna is open year-round, albeit with limited days during the winter, so be sure to check their website first. It is also subject to weather closures in the rainy or wintry season.

For more information see
www.pontetibetanosassodicastalda.com

29. Take a Walk with the Forest in Satriano di Lucania

A walk in the woods is a nice diversion, but this isn't your average hike. In fact, it's the *forest* that does the walking during the Carnevale celebrations in Satriano di Lucania. The *Foresta Che Cammina* is a march of men covered in greenery held the last Sunday before Fat Tuesday.

The ancient anthropomorphic rite begins with men (and some women, let's be fair) transforming themselves into trees, called *U' rumita*, draped in ivy or other foliage. Carrying a cane, they move stealthily through the woods and make their way towards town, an "invasion" of 131 *rumita*, one for every town in Basilicata.

Silently stalking into Satriano, they use their canes to knock on the doors of the houses. Each person graced by the verdant visitor respects the silence and donates a little something –a few coins or a tasty treat.

Once in town they are joined by bears, *orsi*, who have just awakened from hibernation, hopping and dancing through the streets. A shepherd tries to keep them from causing too many problems to the townspeople. Then there is the *quaresima*, a woman dressed in black carrying an empty cradle on her head; she is melancholic and walks slowly, representing the sadness and hardness of life. Yes, folks, this annual rite has a bit of everything. But wait. There's more.

Following the peculiar but lively procession around town, everyone gathers to await *'A Zita*, the bride. A cross-dress ceremony ensues with a man-in-drag "bride" from Satriano and a female-as-groom from nearby Tito, to be wed on the steps of the church. It is a playful renewal of the two towns settling a feud over the Torre di Satriano, situated half-way between them. Yes, it's hilarious.

The *foresta che cammina* represents the personification of the tree spirit and spring rebirth, but now also carries an ecological message to respect the land and the forests.

Don't worry if you can't make it to Satriano for *Carnevale*; you can still walk with the forest (sort of) by strolling among the Neverland-like murals that adorn the town, some of which represent this treasured tradition. There are so many murals here –about 150- that Satriano di Lucania is dubbed "the most painted town in Italy." They certainly make walking around a colorful delight. You can also stroll through the Bosco Spera forest; just be on the look-out for trees that walk.

While You're Here – Why not treat yourself to a lunch that is pleasing to the palate and the eyes? The **Ristorante Sotto La Torre** is an upscale but unpretentious place that serves gorgeous (and tasty) meals that deviate from the "ordinary" menu you usually find in a hill town. It's a special kind of place.

POTENZA

THE CAPITAL CITY

The region's capital, Potenza is dubbed "the vertical city" and it's not hard to see why. It heaves on the sides of the hill, its tall apartment buildings enhancing the vertical effect. Resting at 819 meters above sea level, it's Italy's highest regional capital. Having been rattled many times in its history, the most recent earthquake in 1980 leveled a hefty portion of the city and left dozens of people dead. It also gave Potenza its rather unsightly modern appearance, but the ridge on top does hold the historic center, the more attractive quarter of town.

Up in the old town is where you'll find the cobbled lanes, a pair of interesting museums; don't miss the **National Archeology Museum** as it is exceptionally well-done with its displays covering 10,000 years of history. On the main square, Piazza Mario Pagano, the teensy jewelry-box of a theater, **Teatro Francesco Stabile**, is a gilded and velvet-swathed space with a variety of shows and cultural events. Stop in the **Gran Caffe Italia** for a refreshment and to watch the people parade stroll by. If it's gelato you're after, head up the Via Pretoria (turn right out the door of the Gran Caffe) to **Caruso's**, with the city's best creamy stuff, made on site.

The **cathedral** is dedicated to San Gerardo della Porta, a saint from Piacenza who stopped in Potenza on his way to the Holy Land, and decided to stay. He became bishop, and was credited with healings. But he is remembered most fondly by the Potentini for his part in overturning a Turkish incursion into the territory; as legend holds, it was his intercessory prayers that prevailed to rout the invading forces. The episode is reenacted annually in honor of San Gerardo's feast day (May 29) with a lengthy costumed parade called **La Pirata dei Turchi**.

A word of caution: Potenza is one of the most confusing cities in Italy for drivers. The roads make sense only to those who have been lost in their swirling, poorly-signed midst a few times over. Streets turn back on themselves, become one-way suddenly, and fly-over interchanges are dubbed "spaghetti bowls" by the locals, because in essence, that's what they resemble. Parking is a perennial problem.

The easiest route to the historic center is the escalator system (#30) with accompanying parking deck on Viale dell'Unicef. To reach it, you'll cross the much-acclaimed **Ponte Musmeci**, a stylistic bridge designed by noted engineer Sergio Musmeci. Unfortunately, the road surface on top doesn't let you view the beauty of the structure; for that you have to descend below the bridge. Its graceful, contemporary line was opened in 1975.

The city gives off a harsh face but ask a Potentino for directions, and he's likely to accompany you, chatter along the way, and point out a church or monument, too. Potenza is, after all, the capital of Lucania, where they take to heart the popular saying, "*L'ospitalita' e' sacra*" (hospitality is sacred).

30. Ride Europe's Longest Escalator in Potenza

With the verticality and complicated street network in Potenza, the best way to arrive at the top of town, where the pretty part of the city is located, is via the city's network of escalators. It's sort of like a train-less vertical metro system. It's also the longest in Europe, a point of pride for the Potentini. The *scala mobile* is actually a system of several covered series of escalators and tunnels, with pieces connecting different parts of town.

The longest stretch and most notable, though, is the Santa Lucia portion. One section descends a hill from the so-called Serpentone (big snake) housing block area to the Fondo Valle (valley), with the other, longer primary section ascending the steep hillside up to the city center. The glassed tunnel-like covering gives you a good impression of its length. Inside, it is actually a long snake of connected escalators all in a row. It culminates at an elevator that takes you the final jaunt up to the Santa Lucia district of Potenza's old town.

From there, you cross the street and walk into the *centro storico*, where stone houses, painted *palazzi* and upscale shops are scattered amidst the alleys and main street, Via Pretoria. Up here, you'll find a more classic atmosphere than the hodgepodge of modern buildings that make up the bulk of the city. The **National Archeology Museum** housed in Palazzo Loffredo is a must, with its rich collection of artifacts dating back to the 6th century BC. It includes ornate gold and silver women's jewelry, bronze and iron warriors' helmets and daggers, painstakingly-formed marble and ceramic votives, sculptures, pottery and more, from the Lucani, the Greeks, and Romans. The **cathedral** is dedicated to the city's patron saint, San Gerardo della Porta, who dedicated himself to service to the area as bishop and miracle worker.

The **cathedral** was originally a Romanesque 13th century structure but was restyled in the 1700s to the current neoclassical design you see. Nevertheless, it's a superb symbol of the city and the chapels and altars are from the 1500s. The busy bronze doors tell the story of San Gerardo, with a risen Christ in the middle and the four apostles in the corners. The interior of the dome shows a parade of Potentini with San Gerardo being presented to Mary with a cloud of angels and heavenly father above. Quite a scene, really. The body of the saint himself is entombed in the right-hand chapel, protected by an iron gate.

The humbler **church of San Michele** is closer to the escalator, an older, stone Gothic chapel that highlights its history and is popular for weddings.

While you're up in the *centro*, enjoy a stroll along the Via Pretoria, stopping in one of the many cafes for a drink or coffee break. The best gelato is found here at **Caruso** (it's easy to miss, so look for it at Via Pretoria 204). Oddly, most of the restaurants up here are open only for dinner (**Trattoria del Duomo** is excellent, as is **Ristorante Antiche Torri**). If it's lunch you want, the casual **Peperoncino** across from the museum is a handy choice, or you can have a Neapolitan pizza fresh out of the wood-burning oven at **Noi di Napoli** (Vicolo Bruno 16, closed Monday), just off Via Pretoria, open for lunch as well as dinner.

How to reach the escalator in the first place? Exit the highway at Potenza Centro, cross the bridge and go left through the roundabout, over the "flyover" bridge and along the *fondovalle* (also called Viale del Unicef) until you see the parking garage on your right. There is a charge of 25 cents each way to ride the escalator system.

31. Go Hog Wild and Eat a Piece of History

It's no secret that Italians love all things pig; from north to south, platters of prosciutto and whole-roasted *porchetta* are savored far and wide, by young and old. In Basilicata, they're no different, but they can claim a piece of culinary history that pre-dates the Romans- one that is still proudly produced by families and commercial *salumerie* around the region. My people, I give you, *lucanica*.

It is more than its mere definition as "sausage" would imply, because *lucanica* goes far back in the mists of time and is still made pretty much the same way as it was done when the Lucani people perfected it. When the Romans took over the territory, they took to the sausages of the land, too. In fact, ancient Roman scholar Marco Terenzio Varrone wrote in his history that it was "called *lucanica* by the Roman soldiers because they learned to make it from the Lucani." Cicero and Orazio both waxed nostalgic about the porky treat, which comes as sweet or spicy sausage, and fresh or cured versions. It was so good that it was worth writing home about! The Romans also appreciated that the sausage cured and kept well, making it readily transportable for a road trip meal. One can imagine them pulling off the Via Appia for a roadside picnic, munching on the *lucanica* and bread, with a swig of Aglianico wine (#50).

Real *lucanica* is made from selected pieces of pork and fat, both of which are cut by hand into small cubes (not ground), spiced with salt, pepper, ground *peperone dolce* (#23) and wild fennel seeds. The spicy version adds *piccante* chile powder to the mix.

So now that your taste buds are primed for the pork, where can you eat it? Just about everywhere, really. Salumerie shops, the *braceria*-butcher shops, *agriturismos* and restaurants all over Basilicata proudly make and serve it, so be sure to give it a taste in both the fresh and salami versions.

But if you truly want to go hog wild, then visit one of the two festivals that put the historic pig product at the forefront.

The first is in Cancellara, northeast of Potenza, a town that festoons its patron saint of San Biagio with streamers of sausage links. Saint Blaise's feast day of February 3 is heralded with the Festival of Sausage Chains (*festa della salsiccia a catena*), where, as festival organizers say, "Faith, tradition and taste are found in perfect harmony." Who can resist *that*? Following the Mass and the blessing of the throats, you can swallow down the sausage, made strictly according to the millennia-old preparation method. There's plenty of wine to keep your throat lubricated, too. Cancellara puts on an encore with a sausage festival in September, too.

The second event is an August blow-out called, appropriately, Porklandia. Go to pig-land and get hog wild in Picerno, west of Potenza, a town famous for its various salami products. This annual shindig is dedicated to all things pork –and not just eating, but pig-related art, literature and cooking demonstrations, too. Of course, there are lines of food stands proffering the goods that the festival is celebrating, so you can enjoy it grilled, baked or simmered in sauce, and a dozen other imaginative ways.

So go ahead, pig out on a *lucanica* sausage or two; you're biting into a piece of history!

See Cancellara's city web page for exact dates and details:
www.prolococancellara.simplesite.com

Picerno's Porklandia news is found on their Facebook page:
https://www.facebook.com/Porklandia-173513976160935/

32. At Muro Lucano, Cross that Bridge When You Come to It

It's not hard to see why the pastel-painted town of Muro Lucano needs bridges; it is plopped on a pinnacle above steep ravines and forbidding hills. One gander tells you it's a special place, its sunny southern exposure highlighted by the joyful sherbert colors, with a castle cherry topping. No wonder FAI (Fondo Ambiente Italia) named it one of the *luoghi del cuore* (literally, places of the heart, or unforgettable places). Rome's leading newspaper, La Repubblica, called it a *borgo presepe*, a village nativity scene. With such praises, you know it will be charming.

This seemingly out-of-the-way place is where Basilicata's patron saint, San Gerardo Maiella, was born and raised; where

Queen Giovanna I was assassinated in her preferred castle; where Futurist painter Joseph Stella came from; and where history crossed a bridge.

But first, you should wander around town; you'll find the folks are as sunny and friendly as the pastel appearance would suggest. Definitely walk up to the **castle** with its murderous history; the queen used it as her summer residence but when her conniving cousin claimed his own right to the throne, he imprisoned her here, then sent assassins to finish her reign. Less macabre is the panoramic point above it with 360° eye-popping scenery. Back down in the streets is the **Archeology Museum**, placed in the ex- episcopal seminary; it displays a host of artifacts and is worth a visit to put the ancient eras into perspective.

Now we get to the bridge. And cross it. **The Ponte di Annibale**, or Hannibal's Bridge, is located just outside the current *centro storico* of Muro Lucano, a single-arched stone bridge below the rocky massif. It was on a route that Hannibal and his Carthaginian troops crossed on several occasions as they tried to out-do the Roman legions in several battles, traveling between Calabria, Campania, and northern Puglia. Many historians think this particular bridge was built in 1,000 AD, replacing the original one. It is known that Hannibal clashed with the forces of Marco Claudio Marcello at the nearby settlement of **Numistro** in 210 BC. Did he actually cross this bridge? *Boh*. But you can. It has survived almost miraculously through the many centuries without much care or restoration until recent years, so it is worth the short walk from town. Besides, really, who doesn't like crossing cool stone bridges? (Surely, I'm not the only one.)

Start in Muro's ancient *centro storico*, called **Borgo di Pianello**, which is hidden in the rock around the other side, below the castle. The stair-stepped streets and clustered houses that make up the *borgo* seem frozen in time, and this is where the birthplace home of San Gerardo is found. From there, take the path called **Sentiero delle Rupe** and follow it down, past ruined stone-built water mills and –what else? – walk over that ancient bridge. The path was used for centuries to connect Pianello with the hamlet of Capodigiano and was abandoned at the beginning of the 1900s when the new road was built above.

Which brings us to another bridge to cross. You can see the tall arch of it from Hannibal's bridge; the **Ponte del Pianello** was among the first parabolic bridges of reinforced concrete in Italy. You definitely want to tromp on this one, with its view down into the deep gorge.

Even a short time here shows you that Muro Lucano had a level of prominence that brought many historical figures and happenings to the town. Take the effort to get here. You'll be glad you came and crossed that bridge.

33. Give Your True Love...A Dagger?

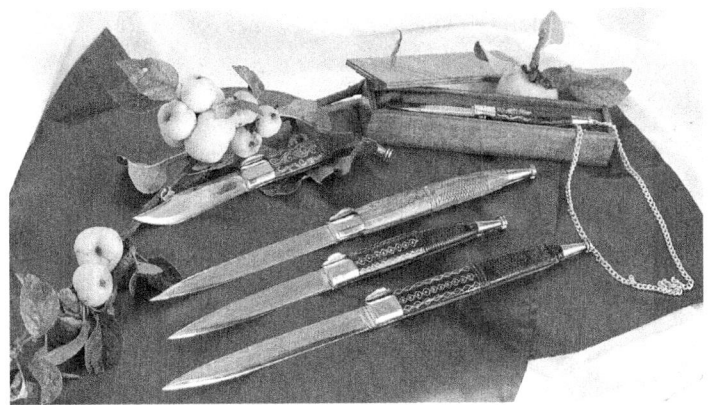

Some men propose with a diamond ring, others on bended knee with loving verses, but in the hilltop town of Avigliano, the men show their marriage intent with a dagger. How romantic!

Avigliano is only 16 kilometers from Potenza but sits in its own world surrounded by mountain peaks where it keeps its own unique dialect. The town enjoyed a prosperous period, as evidenced by the numerous *palazzi* placed around the *centro storico,* and was, for a time, the duchy of the powerful Doria Pamphilj family.

And so it happened, says the murky legend, that the gentlemen of the court first brought their dueling daggers into the area, and local smiths took up the artful production of the unusual cutlery. The nobles would carry one with their coat of arms or other symbols incised into the blade or handle. They were Spanish-style stiletto knives with the three-click opening system of the dueling dagger – the first position was a warning;

the second was a signal of acceptance of the challenge; and the third meant business, opening the dagger into full "let's rumble" position.

The more popular version of the story is also more colorful and explains why the *balestra*, as it is called, became a wedding registry must. The commoners began to carry the daggers for their own protection against both man and beast in the vast wooded mountain territory. The craft of the daggers coincided with the years of feudalism, when the local lord could invoke his self-proclaimed right *to jus primae noctis*, or "first night"- meaning he could take a new bride to his bed chamber on her wedding night to claim her virginity, before sending her home to her new husband. The rebellious Aviglianesi decided to fight back at this overhanded custom, and thus the engagement gift of a *balestra* was born. The betrothed could carry it among her skirts to defend herself if the feudal lord, or any other lecherous low-life, came a'calling.

Even today, the tradition continues and the *balestras* are gifted to Avigliano's brides-to-be. They're made of fine craftsmanship: olive leaf-shaped forged blades with ornate engraving, and carved buffalo or sheep horn handles. They're not hard to spot in the town's shop windows, their protective presence nestled amidst crystal and other wedding registry items.

While you're in Avigliano, be sure to get your fill of the town's specialty that brings in folks from all over the area (#34).

Want to buy a *balestra* for your *amore*? Count on spending at least €800 for the handmade daggers, though prices can go over €1,200 depending on the materials and incising designs.

You can go to the source and meet the artisans; three continue the craft tradition.

Canio Coviello; Via San Michele Fuori le Mura, 6.
Phone: (+39) 334-665-373.

Vito Aquila; Via Don Nicola Stolfi.
Phone: (+39) 335-834-4029. www.vitoaquila.it

Vito Summa; Phone: (+39) 339-403-8311.
Facebook page: Balestra Aviglianese

34. Bring On The Baccalà

Dried salt cod that looks like slabs of weathered barn wood may seem an unlikely food to get excited about, but people in these parts go mad for the reconstituted fish called *baccalà*. Indeed, it is popular all through the south, but especially in the inland hinterlands.

In the days before refrigeration, fresh fish was scarce in mountain communities but salted cod could be transported by traveling *commercianti* and kept indefinitely. It could be set aside in a *cantina* and brought out for special occasions, or for Friday Lenten meals. For decades it was considered a "peasant food," but in recent years it has found its place among more refined palates and trendy chefs as a gourmet treat (and thus, its price has risen, too).

The town of Avigliano is especially renowned for its creativity and specialized preparations in all things *baccalà*. It's said that the residents here have hundreds of ways of making the dried fish not just edible, but laudable. Folks come from neighboring regions just to sample the Aviglianese styles of preparing it, and thousands descend on the town every August for its annual Sagra del Baccalà festival.

You don't have to plan your visit around the annual event, though, as the restaurants around Avigliano serve it up in varied and imaginative forms all year long. Most have a complete menu that revolves entirely around cod fish, from the *antipasto* to the *primo* and *secondo*, and, in some cases, right on through to dessert! (Yes, it's true; I saw a tiramisú of *baccalà* on a menu. I wasn't that brave. Give it a try and let me know how it is!)

The most popular and regional of dishes is the *baccalà* with *peperoni cruschi*, the crispy sweet peppers that the region is famous for (#23), crumbled on it as a main course with potatoes, or as a *primo piatto* combined with hand-formed *strascinati* pasta. But you'll find a cornucopia of the stuff, in ways you could never have imagined, with the chefs so skilled you don't realize the basis of the delicacies is...well, dried and reconstituted cod fish.

My personal recommendations are Ristorante Gagliardi, in the heart of Avigliano, or Osteria del Borgo, on the upper edge of town, but there are several restaurants to choose from, and *baccalà* is certain to be the centerpiece of the menu, so sit yourself down and tell them to "Bring it on!"

An added bonus: Osteria del Borgo is also a Buon Ricordo restaurant; when you order their house specialty (with *baccalà* of course!) you take home a hand-painted commemorative plate. Osteria Gagliardi is easy to find right off the main street, but ask anyone and they will surely show you where to eat!

See: http://www.osteriaalborgo.com/ and
http://www.osteriagagliardi.it/index.jsf

While You're Here

If you happen to come in August, the Sagra del Baccala isn't the only highlight. Avigliano presents a pretty amazing event called **I Quadri Plastici**, which doesn't even begin to describe what happens. Teams get together to recreate famous art scenes in living glory. Each year has a designated theme. The detail, lighting, and poses are nothing short of extraordinary. It takes place the first Sunday of August.

35. JOIN A BAND OF BRIGANDS

There are brigands in Basilicata, and they put on one helluva performance. Every weekend from the beginning of August through mid-September the era of *i briganti* comes to life at the Parco Grancia outside tiny Brinidisi di Montagna.

In a huge open-air, natural amphitheater below town, Il Parco Storico La Grancia is a multi-venue historical theme park with six areas for education, theatre, music and art. There is Il Borgo, a sort of Lucanian frontier-town where artisans in period costumes demonstrate traditional crafts, and -this being Italy- there are several stands and restaurants where you can eat locally-produced delicacies that would have been served during the turbulent years of *brigantaggio*, the late 1800s. Music and dance performances are designed to reflect the area's unique history and culture.

But the main event of this park is La Storia Bandita, a grand production dubbed as a "*cine-spettacolo*". It is a beautiful blending of impassioned live performance, dramatically-devised video projection, and astounding special effects, utilizing the bare cliff wall opposite and the ruins of the 11th century castle perched above Brindisi. Seriously, this is one amazing show.

Interestingly, La Storia Bandita means "the history of the bandits" but could also be translated as "banned history". It is a clever word play for the period when many Lucani felt that their culture and history had been marginalized, trivialized and tyrannized. Tired of invasions and overly dominating landowners that kept them poor, oppressed and disillusioned, the period of the Risorgimento (the unification of Italy) proved to be a flashpoint for many southern peasants who joined together and formed a band of bandits. They became known as *briganti*.

La Storia Bandita tells a dramatized version of this period, focusing on the charismatic leader of the pack, Carmine Crocco, who was called the General of the Briganti. From events in his childhood to cynicism with the unification forces, the story shows how and why the *briganti* took things into their own hands in an attempt to protect their lands and traditions from what they viewed as an invasion by foreign rulers.

The production is astounding, with hundreds of participants in an all-volunteer cast and crew. Dance and music reflect the rural Lucanian life at the time. Crocco authored an autobiography and some of his rousing prose is movingly recited. But the effects! When the forces invade, the castle is set aflame. Gunfire echoes loudly in the canyon and the flashes illuminate the mountain formations. Images are projected behind the set on the rock. A water-wall shoots up in a stirring finale.

You don't have to understand much Italian to follow the show. The performances play it all out before your eyes. This is a production worth seeing.

More information: www.parcograncia.it

36. Star Gazing and Arabian Nights in Pietrapertosa

You won't find desert sands or Aladdin's lamp in Pietrapertosa, but you will find a magic carpet of constellations in the sky and the exotic atmosphere of Arabian nights. The stars you can see year-round, thanks to the town's status as Basilicata's highest community. The Arabian nights...well, that happens only in August.

I can hear you asking what Arabia could possibly have to do with a remote village on a mountaintop in Basilicata, Italy. I'm coming to that. But first: In the beginning there were the Greeks. They came several centuries BC and gave the town some place names that are still in use, like "la costa di Diana". Then came the Romans. And then the Goths and the Lombards. And then things got interesting.

In 838 an Arab contingent arrived inland from the Metaponto plains, led by a certain King Bomar who established a fortress-town among the craggy peaks of the Dolomiti Lucane mountains at 1,100 meters above sea level (3,609 feet). From here they controlled a vast territory and fought to keep the Byzantines at bay. Even after their domination ended, their presence remained and intermingled with the native inhabitants, as well as the Normans and Spanish and others who arrived later. They also left Arabic influences in the dialect and foods. Even now, you can see some Middle Eastern traces in the eyes and faces of the townspeople. Indeed, the neighboring town of Castelmezzano, visible across the deep gorge, had a different history that was tied to the Normans. They looked at Pietrapertosa with a suspicion that became so ingrained that still today, despite the passing centuries and their common zip line and hiking paths, the folks in Castelmezzano will wave off mentions of their mountaintop neighbors with a dismissive comment that "they're all Arabs over there." (For their part, the Pietrapertosani smack-talk the Castelmezzanesi, too.)

The *rione Arabata*, the Arab Quarter, is still standing, the oldest and highest district of town. Its steep labyrinth of narrow stair-stepped lanes weave around the houses built right onto the rock. It's unchanged through the centuries and will surely challenge your climbing skills.

The district comes alive every August to celebrate their Arab heritage with a two-day festival, Sulle Tracce degli Arabi (In the footsteps of the Arabs). The mystical Arabian Nights are evocative with richly-flavored foods, exotic music and dancing, along with shows and street artists.

As for the celestial gazing, that's easy because on any clear night the mantle of stars is so close and so clear that you can practically trace the constellations with your finger. Pietrapertosa is the highest town in Basilicata, after all. Bands of the Milky Way are usually visible from here, so this is the perfect spot for romantics and naked-eye astronomy geeks (you know who you are). In fact, Pietrapertosa is so well known for its stargazing that a local *albergo diffuso* ("scattered hotel") is called Le Costellazioni, with each suite named for (you guessed it) a constellation.

So, whether you want to walk in the footsteps of the Arabs, or set your sights on the stars (or both), a night or two in Pietrapertosa will fulfill your dreams.

While you're here, why not fly with the angels, too? (#37)

37. Fly with the Angels at Castelmezzano

Arriving in Castelmezzano amidst the craggy peaks and spires of the Dolomiti Lucane mountains, set off against the striking blue sky, certainly puts you in a celestial frame of mind. The town is a visual feast and looks less like it was built and more like it miraculously grew out of the surrounding rocks. It certainly seems like angels might alight here as a resting spot.

Castelmezzano exudes mystery and antiquity. The town was a Norman stronghold named "middle castle" because it was placed between the two castle fortresses of Pietrapertosa and Brindisi Montagna. Founded by folks who were fleeing Saracen raids further down the Basento valley, they couldn't have chosen a more isolated spot to settle among the crags and clefts of the rocks. It remained in a world almost of its own, like its sister town across the deep ravine, Pietrapertosa, until after WWII when the road was built. Before that, mule paths connected it to other towns.

The folks of Castelmezzano looked a bit askew at their counterparts over on the other peak, their Norman and Templar mindsets not fully trusting of the Arab-descended inhabitants of Pietrapertosa (#36). But times change, and the two towns put aside their centuries-long rivalry to join together (literally) when they built the Volo dell'Angelo zip line. Forget those piddly sit-down lines that scurry among the trees, though. This one is an open-air thrill ride strung between the two towns, with two 4,000-feet long cables spanning a 1,200 feet deep gorge. The ride launches you at 120 kilometers per hour over gorgeous scenery in one breathtaking minute of invigorating free-flight sensation.

The full-on adrenaline rush somehow seems serene and tranquil as you watch the folds of the landscape, the sheep grazing below and birds flying above, all while soaring at high speed. It is a round-trip flight so you get to experience it twice on one ticket!

Reserve online in advance during the months of July and August, when it draws peak crowds. Now, a few details. As mentioned, it is a round-trip flight, because once you get to the opposite town, you have to get back again. Second, the departure point is outside of town up on the mountain. A shuttle will take you to the "end of the road" but from there, it's a 20-minute hike; bring water. In Pietrapertosa, the arrival point is below town; from there is a shuttle takes you in to the village. You'll have to walk through town and up along the rock where the castle once stood to reach the launch spot, easier than in Castelmezzano, but the steep climb still leaves you a bit breathless. It is worthwhile to spend some time and take in the town, maybe have lunch or a gelato before flying back.

Castelmezzano strings along the mountain following the natural curve the landscape, with archways, steps and lanes to explore. It's all very picturesque. Walk all the way along and then uphill toward the crest where you can see the old footholds in the rock that once led to a look-out point. From the ridge you can look east and on a clear day see six hill towns sprinkled along the route towards the Ionian Sea.

The main church in the piazza looks ordinary but hides some Templar symbols (#51). The town crest still shows two Templars on a horse. Castelmezzano doesn't have 'tourist sights' but has a lot of Old World atmosphere and you'll easily see why it's been named one of the "prettiest villages in Italy" *(i borghi piu' belli d'Italia)*.

Prefer to stay rooted on the ground? No problem! There's still adventure to be had while you wait for your angel-flying friends. You can still visit Pietrapertosa by way of the **Sette Pietre Trail** (meaning seven stones), a three-kilometer path that descends the gorge and then ascends (steeply) to Pietrapertosa. It's dotted with seven stone sculptures along the way.

If that's too much walking, then how about an adrenaline rush while sitting down? The folks at Dolomiti Discovery offer fun ATV tours of the area, taking you through varied landscapes and panoramic points; all you have to do is sit tight and hang on!

Even if you don't fly the Volo dell'Angelo (though you *should*!) you can walk to the top of town or along the path to the launch site and watch those who do, so you can truly say you've seen angels in flight.

More Information: Volo dell'Angelo website:
https://www.volodellangelo.com/index_eng.asp (in English)

Dolomiti Discovery:
http://www.dolomitidiscovery.it/en (Also in English)

The Sette Pietre Trail:
http://www.volodellangelo.com/eng/web/item.asp?nav=48

38. Get Fired Up at Italy's Largest Bonfire

I can't overlook my own town, because while it may not have any tourist sights, it does have a claim to fame that is fun for everyone. The tiny town of Trivigno in central Basilicata throws an annual blow-out to celebrate the feast day of Sant'Antonio Abate and sets ablaze the biggest bonfire in Italy.

The normally-sleepy village of 600 draws visitors from around Basilicata and neighboring regions to see the monstrous pile of wood in the piazza and to partake in the midwinter party that lasts as long as the embers do. That usually means the next day, but it's been known to simmer for two days, and beyond.

The tradition's beginnings are lost in time, but St. Anthony the Abbot has been celebrated here for centuries, the kindly protector of animals called upon by the rural inhabitants to safeguard their flocks and herds. The *festa* starts with the religious rites –a Mass, the igniting of a small fire and the blessing of the animals; nowadays mostly domestic pets are brought to the church for the benediction. After that, a flame is taken to set alight the behemoth bonfire in the primary piazza. And that's when the bacchanalia begins.

Live music, a line-up of food booths, street entertainment and plenty of dancing around the fire keep the party blazing all night, warmed by the flames and the flowing wine, as well as the energetic *pizzica* folk dance that is revered by all ages around these parts. Regional favorites like *lagane e ceci* (fat pasta pieces with chickpeas), grilled *lucanica* sausages (#31), and the thing that gets my mouth watering, *caciocavallo podicolico* (#40) *impiccato*, meaning hung over the coals to get melty. Then it's slathered on a slab of grilled bruschetta; it is heaven on toast. Nutella crepes and other sweets keep the energy levels high.

The *festa* is called *La notte dei Falo e dei Desideri*; that it is to say, the Night of the Bonfires and of Wishes. *Desideri* because another longstanding tradition tied to Sant'Antuon, as he is called in these parts, is to write down your deepest desires, then burn it in the flames. Along with that, here they launch paper lanterns to send your wishes up to the sky, first writing your wish on it, of course.

This party is a *notte bianca* (literally, white night, meaning all-nighter) so come and get your groove on: eat, drink and dance 'til dawn to banish those mid-winter blues.

The *Festa di Sant'Antonio e dei Desideri* in Trivigno is held on the Saturday closest to the saint day, which is January 16. If you're going to be in Italy in winter, it is great fun and a *festa* few tourists experience, so check the dates and come dance with me; we'll get fired up around the biggest bonfire in Italy!

39. Gaze at the Heavens – and Some Heavenly Art

Higher to the heavens, the mountain-top town of Anzi sits at more than 1,000 meters (3,280 feet) above sea level, the second-highest town in Basilicata. The leg-challenging streets are so steep that some of them have chain handrails along them to grab onto when they are icy or slick. Staggering up the side of Mt. Siri, the pretty old town culminates in a mirage-like sight at the top –the gleaming metal dome of an astronomical observatory and planetarium.

But first, meander through town and visit the **church of Santa Lucia**, dating to the 1100s. I tell you this because taking it slowly will make it less fatiguing on your legs. Stop in for a drink at one of the bars to catch your breath, and if the permanent exhibit **multi-scene nativity** is open, be sure to take a look. It is a beauty, with various hand-detailed representations of the life of Jesus with the unique backdrops of Basilicata landscapes and monuments worked in. It's really a masterpiece. (Look for the signs indicating ***Presepe Poliscenico***.)

Now, back to those steep streets to huff it up to the top and the silvery cupola that lets you see the heavens. The planetarium was placed here at this lofty town for its lack of light pollution and incredibly clear skies.

There is a monthly line-up of events that revolves around the astronomical and lunar phenomenon occurring each month. Special events have included food and wine, special lectures based on Pythagoras (#7), space specialist Rocco Petrone (#28), and poetry under the stars. A*peritivi* and pizza nights are part of their program, too. Check the monthly calendar at www.dreaminglucania.it.

The guys and gals who run it are science or art experts and have loads of enthusiasm for the projects and the town. They'll also speak English to explain it to you and involve you in the events.

But what about the art, you ask? While the array of stars is certainly a work of art, next door to the planetarium is the seemingly spare church known as Santa Maria di Monte Siri. But that's the exterior's impression. Crack open the door, though, and you're in for an eye-popping surprise because it is fancifully frescoed, and you just don't expect it. I will save some of the surprises contained in the paintings for your visit, but the gorgeous works were done around 1559 by Giovanni

Todisco, from nearby Abriola. Like many of his better-known contemporaries, Todisco worked local flora and landmarks into his scenes; I especially love the *caciocavallo* (see #40) hanging at the nativity. In rare artistic rendering, he also paints apocryphal scenes.

To see it, you'll have to schedule a tour, as the church is only used for Mass during the month of May (when you might be lucky enough to find it unlocked). Otherwise, it is definitely worth your while to reserve the visit, as these frescoes from the 1550s are really something special to see.

Through DreamingLucania.it you can organize tours of the observatory, the church, and the nativity scene *presepe poliscenico*. Or, just send an email to planetarioanzi@gmail.com. You can also drive to the top of town beyond the cemetery rather than climbing the steep streets.

Anzi is located about 25 kilometers south of Potenza along the SS 92 road, a truly beautiful drive.

40. Taste One of Italy's Most Prized (and Priciest) Cheeses in Abriola

Apologies to the vegans among us, but I love cheese. Always have. Here in Basilicata we have several swoon-worthy varieties, but the best, in my opinion, is the region's acclaimed *caciocavallo podolico*.

A cow's milk cheese made from the mountain-grazing *podolico* breed of cattle, *caciocavallo podolico* from Basilicata is one of Italy's most acclaimed and most expensive cheeses. Bearing the aromas and flavors of the forest herbs and nuts they graze, this cheese isn't used in cooking so much as it is savored.

Now, *cacio* just refers to cheese, and *cavallo* means horse, which leads to some confusion. It's not horse cheese (though you may have guessed so after reading #6). The name comes from the shape. Two of the pear-shaped forms are tied with a rope, one at each end, and suspended over a beam to age. Hanging this way, in Italian, is called "*a cavallo*" (like saddlebags on a horse).

One more thing (my pride knows no bounds): it's not to be confused with "ordinary" *caciocavallo*, which is produced in neighboring regions. Because it's the *podolico* milk that makes it truly special. Because this breed is free-range in the mountains and produces a smaller quantity of milk than others, it costs more. And because the concentrated flavors in that milk are what give the cheese its complexity and flavor.

Caciocavallo podolico can be found in various stages of aging – from a few months to several years. It gets sharper and richer as it ages. But the flavor actually varies based on the season when the cheese is made, because of those grazing herbs change by period; winter brings a more delicate fragrance and flavor, while spring flowers and grasses are more forward and stronger.

It's a worthy splurge, in my opinion, but taste it for yourself and see. A true pasture-grazed and hand-made *caciocavallo podolico* costs from €60-70 a kilogram if it's aged four months or so, and goes up to €90 and more for those aged two to three years. (That comes out to about $220 per pound!)

Eat it plain, but it's especially delicious when drizzled with local chestnut honey. However. My favorite way to enjoy it is a local specialty that evokes the Meg Ryan diner reaction (you know the one, from When Harry Met Sally). *Caciocavallo podolico impiccato* is found at the local festivals where the saddlebag-shaped cheese is suspended over hot coals and the melted creaminess is slathered on toasted bruschetta. Yes, yes, yes.

Where to taste it? You can go to the source at Azienda Pessolani in mountaintop **Abriola**, where the cool cheese-aging grotto and tasting room will give you a glimpse and a sampling of the glories of this cheese. See: www.caseuscafe.it

If you can't make it to Abriola, the conveniently-located (but less charming) Latteria Salvia in **Tito** also makes a mean *caciocavallo podolico*, among other cheeses. They have a location in the historic center of Potenza, as well. See: www.latteriasalvia.it

41. Time Travel with the Holy Roman Emperor in Lagopesole

While Melfi (#48) was a seat of power and summer residence for the court of Frederick II, the Holy Roman Emperor and King of Sicily, he built many castles throughout the area, from curiously mysterious like the Castel del Monte in nearby Puglia, to mild-mannered and stately, like the one here in Castel Lagopesole. It sits on hill (of course, don't they all?) and would have been surrounded by thick woods back in 1242 when Fredrick took over a smaller Norman castle and ordered significant renovations.

The brick structure is rectangular with low but thick corner towers and two interior courtyards. It became the ruler's favorite hunting lodge, and its regal rooms hosted dignitaries and the emperor's family. The castle is often referred to as a manor house because of its residential nature, though a section was devoted to defenses and Frederick's guard. The courtyard would have seen sumptuous banquets, what with all that game and fowl that the emperor loved hunting for. It was certainly large and attractive but fairly simple in its design.

Or, maybe not so simple after all. The emperor's beloved castle was the only one of his many royal holdings with a chapel built into it. That leaves some people pondering; couple that with the strangely-placed off-center and angled tower in the second courtyard and you have some serious head-scratching. There may be some mysterious symbolism here known only to Frederick II. Or is it something else? Those of you chasing down Templar lore and symbols (#51) may want to visit Castel Lagopesole to contemplate these anomalies.

The castle is fascinating to explore, because it has been largely left in its original state without too much modern intervention hindering our imaginations from seeing it through the mists of time.

I like to walk the salons and look from the windows and think of the centuries that have passed by this place. But you don't have to imagine too much, because here the stones speak, as they say. **Il Mondo di Federico II** is a series of multimedia surround-vision 3-D projections that immerse you in the realm of the man called the *stupor mundi*, or wonder of the world. The imaginative *museo narrante* puts you inside a kaleidoscope of the politics, passions, science, and intelligence that marked the unique ruler. (In the summer months, an additional spectacular show takes place in the courtyard.) Audio guides are available in English.

If you're lucky enough to come during the second weekend of August, there are events that will knock your socks off. **Alla Corte di Federico** is a theatrical and special effects show that brings the court of Lagopesole to life in costumes, falconry and knights in armor. The **Palio dei Tre Feudi** is a sumptuous costumed affair of Frederick II's multi-ethnic court and medieval games of skill.

Inside the castle is another original museum, dedicated to Basilicata emigration. The **Museo dell'Emigrazione Lucana** will be of interest to anyone of Italian descent. It takes you on a journey that our ancestors did – from the old world to the new world, in photos, films, displays, and interactive exhibits.

For more information see the Facebook pages Museo Narrante Lagopesole and Museo dell'Emigrazione Lucana. There is curiously a lack of information online for such an epic locale.

If you're searching for roots in Basilicata, a stop at the Museo dell'Emigrazione is interesting. If you want to delve in more deeply, my husband Bryan and I are professional genealogists and can assist; see My Bella Basilicata for details. (www.mybellabasilicata.com)

More information: https://www.prolocolagopesole.it (Italian)

42. Visit Albania in the Heart of Basilicata

Southern Italy is a true melting pot, a beautiful fondue of blended cultures that contribute so much to the ceremonies, dialects and facial features of the people –from the indigenous Lucani to the Romans, and the host of rulers and invaders that passed through and left their mark. (See the timeline for more information.) That's why Italian-Americans' genealogical DNA results can sometimes be a little funky, showing French, Spanish, Middle Eastern and Germanic ties that they weren't expecting.

But the Albanians were different. They came to Basilicata and other regions of the south in the 1400s and 1500s following the conquest of the Byzantine Empire by the Ottomans. They sought and found refuge across the Adriatic in Italy and settled in. With the death of their commander, Gjergj Kastrioti Skanderberg, the resistance to the Ottomans succumbed to their invasions, and a large part of the populace fled the Turks. Not only did they settle, they established towns and put down their Albanian roots deeply, and those roots are still flourishing.

They retained many elements of their Greek rite traditions, and the *Arbëreshë* language they brought with them has been frozen in time here, still spoken mostly as it was in the 1400s, an amazing feat and one that attracts linguists from Albania and Greece (and elsewhere) to study it. You can see the language on street signs, which in most of the Albanian towns are written in both *Arbëreshë* and Italian. By the way, their name for Albania was *Arberi*, which is why the people, language, and their communities are called *Arbëreshë*.

There are five towns in Basilicata that keep the flame burning, where you can taste the foods, hear the language, and see the costumes of an ethnic community from long-ago that never fully melted into the southern Italian fondue pot. Three are in the Vulture area (#47), and two are at the gateway of the Pollino National Park (#20).

Maschito. The name derives from *maschio*, male, and indeed Maschito (Masquiti in Arbëreshë) was an all-male settlement of mercenaries who were given the territory by the King of Naples for services rendered. It is said they then brought in women from nearby Venosa and a town was born. Always a bit rebellious the *Maschitani* took an antifascist stand in September, 1943 by declaring themselves the Republic of Maschito, which lasted only a few weeks but set them up clearly as part of the resistance.

Maschito is a wine city and puts on some excellent festivals, so do check the calendar of events during your travels. In particular, **La Retnes** in August, a costumed re-enactment of the *Arbëreshë* against the Ottomans. Also, there is a particularly great food experience here (see the list at the back of the book).

Barile, which means barrel, tells you everything: *vino*! Sitting below Monte Vulture, the town is famous for the rock-hewn cantinas at the edge of town, many of which are still used. It's also one of the *Arbëreshë* towns with some of the most fascinating traditions, like the Holy Week ceremonies that introduce a colorful, dancing *zingara* (gypsy) and her child to the procession. It is she who carries the stakes for the crucifixion hidden in a basket. More light-hearted is the **Tumar me tuluz Festival** in October dedicated to the *Arbëreshë* foods. The cutest tradition is the very old Baptism of the Dolls on June 24, where girls of town put homemade dolls on the street below a step, and hop over them three times. There are cookies, dancing and song after.

Ginestra is known as the *borgo dei sapori*, the village of flavors. And hoo-yah, are they right. Part of the Aglianico zone (#50), the wine is excellent to accompany the hand-made *tagliatelle* pasta with wild fennel (swoon) or *does* (pronounced dos) with tomato sauce, nutmeg, pork steaks and basil topped with local pecorino. Oh, yes. Taste them at La Casareccia restaurant. Or, even better, the Sagra of Sapori in October, an *Arbëreshë* food festival.

San Paolo Albanese garners the title of smallest town in Basilicata, with just 253 residents. But the town is big on its heritage –so big that many of the women still wear the traditional garb while sitting in their doorways making lace and needlework and chatting in *Arbëreshë* dialect. The festival for their patron saint, San Rocco, is something to see, involving sickles and bundles of wheat along with ritual dances and a party that involves all the residents and any visitors who happen by. An open-air art installation called Sky Cleaners is part of the Arte Pollino (#21) inspired by the town's use of Spanish Broom for textiles.

San Costantino Albanese is sort of the epicenter town of *Arbëreshë* culture where the **Etnomuseo della Cultura Arbëreshë** introduces you to the costumes, musical instruments and bygone way of life of the *Arbëreshë* community. On May 2 they have an, um, unusual ceremony connected to the **Madonna della Stella festivities:** they explode three life-size puppets placed on a stage outside the church at the moment the statue of the Madonna is carried outside. Why? *Boh*. More traditional, if you're lucky enough to see one, is the Greek rite wedding ceremony that is still observed here.

A big attraction is the **Volo dell'Aquila**, a mechanical hang-glider that lets you "fly" on a cable. It's a tame attraction for those too chicken to do the Volo dell'Angelo (#37). San Costantino is also a jumping-off point for the spectacular Pollino National Forest (#20).

43. Surround Yourself with Saints in Ripacandida

Called "the land of saints and brigands" you can probably guess it's not the townspeople who are the saints (though they are certainly welcoming to visitors). During the period of *brigantaggio* (1860-1870) the wooded hills, lonely canyons and hidden caves gave refuge to the brigands who rose up against Garibaldi's invasion and the ensuing occupation by the Piemontese troops. (#35)

The saints, on the other hand, are found in the Gothic-style 11th century sanctuary of San Donato. San Donato himself was born here in Ripacandida in 1179, called San Donato da Ripacandida or Donatello, to distinguish him from San Donato of Arezzo. But, that's just a (possibly) interesting side note, because the saints you want to see are inside the sanctuary. Ready?

Walk inside and prepare to be amazed. I almost hate to describe it, because it's great fun to let visitors enter and drop their jaws. The interior is splashed with frescoes from top to bottom, in uber-vibrant detail. So impressive are they that the Santuario di San Donato has been dubbed "little Assisi" since they have a Giotto-like quality to them. The church and the next-door monastery are also of the Franciscan order, and so the sanctuary has further been linked to the famous basilica in Assisi as a "sister church".

But those saints playing out their stories all over the walls and ceiling! Gah! From the Old and New Testaments, they're there, along with St. Francis receiving the stigmata. While some say they were completed by an unknown artist who studied with Giotto, other art history experts believe that two Basilicata artists carried out the works: the Genesis scenes and old testament saints, along with St. Francis, they say, were done by Nicola da Novi, while the new testament scenes were done by Antonio Palumbo of Chiaromonte.

What matters is someone set himself (or themselves) to creating a large-scale masterpiece that still leaves visitors amazed all these centuries later, and allows us to walk inside and surround ourselves with the saints and their stories in a stunning way.

More information and contacts are found at http://www.santuariosandonato.it (In Italian). You can find a useful map of the frescoes to indicate the scenes here: http://www.sandonatoripacandida.net/winopen/winopen/PIANTA.htm, in Italian but easily decipherable.

The Santuario di San Donato was named a "messenger of culture and peace monument" by UNESCO in 2010. Next door is the monastery with a courtyard garden for quiet contemplation. The so-called monumental trees include, strangely enough, a giant sequoia.

While you're here, pop around the cute village and be sure to taste the *ruciulatieggh*, a hard-to-pronounce name for their fennel-studded braided bread. Ripacandida also sits within the Aglianico del Vulture wine zone, so sip some *vino* at Eubea winery or Eleano winery, both on the same provincial road outside town in the area called Piano dell'Altare (again with the saintly theme!).

44. Cool Down in the Cascades at San Fele

One of the best swimming holes in Basilicata is beneath the antique town of San Fele, in the northwest part of the region, near the Campania border. The sweet water flows from the Bradano River (BRAH-dah-no) and converges with two other streams, making this a paradise of natural beauty and cooling pools.

A series of cascades tumble into ponds, some large enough to soak and swim, with a variety of waterfalls to delight the eyes and senses. Who can resist the leaping water plunging and splashing? (Not. Me.)

San Fele reclines along a saddle on a mountain, a true up-and-down town that keeps you fit. As you approach, San Fele is a striking sight. Up close, you get to find out what your legs are made of. One section of town is wrapped around the peak, so to reach it you either have to huff it uphill, downhill and around, or drive a winding road. In fact, there are many trails in the hills to keep hikers satisfied for a week, even apart from the paths to the waterfalls.

But it is the cascades, or *cascate* (kah-SCAH-tay), that San Fele is famous for. Thanks to the efforts of a team of volunteers who maintain the trails and promote the place, it is gaining more attention, at least around southern Italy. Those in the know love the cool river water on a hot summer's day. But it is late spring that they're really gorgeous, with the mountain run-off and spring rains feeding the falls and creating watery works of art. They range from steep and high shooters to lower, gentler cascades. Some crash into the river while others form pools.

There are nine distinct waterfalls, so you can pick and choose, or visit them all, depending on how much time you have, or your stamina. Some are short five- or ten-minute walks, while others will require an hour or more to reach. For example, if you're just interested in a quick view, you can walk a half-mile to the Paradiso falls, or the mere 300 meters to the one called Le Gemelle, which I highly recommend, as it is a convergence of two. Gemelle means "twins" so one of the flows comes from the Acquafredda stream and the other from the Bradano River, two waterfalls on separate rocks that both feed the lovely little lake below. If you're really pressed for time, a three-minute walk takes you to the lofty U'Vertone falls.

The more time you can give it, the better, though. Spend an hour or two walking the U'Vertone path that continues on past that first leaping fall and follows the river to the U'Uattenniere and Innamorati (lovers) falls. From there, you can either retrace your steps, grab the shuttle bus (late spring and summer), or continue on for another 10 minutes to reach the Paradiso and/or Gemelle (twins) falls. Real enthusiasts can walk the path Il Ponte, a four-hour hike that loops through varied landscapes, under a graceful arched bridge, and hits six cascades along the way. By the way, the name given to the entire site is U'Uattenniere, a dialect word for *gualchiere*, the machinery used to run the water-powered mills that once sat along the falls. You'll see the ruins of two of them as you walk.

No matter which path you choose, you can't go wrong. You'll find a magical display of nature's watery spectacle and the chance to jump in and cool down in the naturally-formed pools or stand in the showery mist. What are you waiting for? All in!

More information:
http://www.cascatedisanfele.it (Italian only)

45. Seize The Day In Venosa

The city of Orazio (Horace) as well as a wine destination, Venosa retains its Roman footprint and many ancient reminders of the empire's colony here. Plus, it's just darn attractive with a centerpiece castle, pretty piazzas, shiny-smooth streets, and charm everywhere you look.

It was a Samnite settlement dedicated to the goddess Venere (Venus) when the Romans arrived and conquered in 291 BC. There's a prehistoric site a few kilometers outside the city called Notarchirico, the oldest in Basilicata. The paleolithic park is unfortunately closed to the public. (Access is granted occasionally by beseeching the *comune* by written request.)

Wandering the city is like a scavenger hunt –be on the lookout for the Roman relics, carvings and inscriptions scattered around the *centro storico*. The archeological park at the edge of town is where you can revel in ruins; located on the Via Appia, there are remains of the baths, homes, an amphitheater (across the street), an early Christian-era baptistry, and the hauntingly beautiful Incompiuta church (#46).

Roman Venusia was a flourishing town when Orazio Flacco was born in 65 BC. The writer became a popular poet, and his fame still resonates today; even if you don't know of him, we have him to thank for the "seize the day" sentiment. "Seize the day, put very little trust in tomorrow (the future)".

You can visit the **Casa di Orazio**, an interesting look into a humble Roman home. Don't miss the **Castello Ducale**, an imposing and controversial structure. A cathedral had occupied the space but was torn down in 1443 by Pirro del Balzo, duke of Venosa, to build the castle. The moat and drawbridge were nice defensive touches, perhaps to help keep out the angry townspeople who had to wait until 1512 to get another cathedral consecrated. There are intriguing relics in the museum, including Hebrew inscribed plaques from Venosa's once-thriving Jewish community in the Middle Ages. In fact, there are a series of **Jewish catacombs** outside town, unfortunately open only rarely. The *castello* got a re-do in the mid-1500s to make it a more regal residence, adding the lovely loggias in the courtyard that you can enjoy during your visit

The church of **San Rocco** is the small chapel you can see at the opposite end of the archeology area (#46). It was originally built in 1503 when the town was being besieged by the plague, in hopes that the saint would save them from the scourge. He was named a patron saint and good Venosa still reveres him with an annual procession and party that lasts a week, as befitting the saving grace the devoted population feels St. Rocco bestows on them.

Be sure to sample some of the famed **Aglianico del Vulture** here. You can visit one (or more) of the wineries for a more atmosphere-filled tasting of the region's only DOCG-status *vino*. (#50)

Venosa is also among *i borghi piu' belli d'Italia* (most beautiful villages of Italy), so it goes without saying that wandering the streets will be an eye-pleasing experience. It's also tasty, because the restaurants here serve excellent Lucanian fare. Go ahead; seize the day – in Venosa, "Eat, drink, and be merry" has been the mantra for more than two millennia.

To really immerse yourself, stay in town for a night or two. It's an excellent base for seeing northern Basilicata. If you really want to go in-depth, the gals of Minutiello Viaggi provide guide services to Venosa and other towns around the area to reveal more of the hidden aspects of these fascinating places.

More Information: https://www.minutielloviaggi.com

46. Cross the Abbey Road in Venosa

At the edge of Venosa sits the largest monastic complex in Basilicata, where you get three churches in one. Even better, you get to wander through fascinating Roman remains and have some mystery thrown in for better intrigue.

First up, the Antica Chiesa, or old church, which oddly enough is the one still in use, while the ancient-looking shell of the Incompiuta is actually the Chiesa Nuova. Confused? Let me explain.

At the Abbazia della Santissima Trinita on the edge of Venosa, the old church was supposed to be expanded. Its origins go to a paleo-Christian church built in the 1st century. Then a church was built at the cuff of the 5th and 6th centuries where a Roman pagan temple had stood. It had a single nave with transept, and was then expanded under the Normans. But less than a century later it was decided that a larger church was needed, and construction began on the Chiesa Nuova, behind the existing structure.

And that's where things get interesting. There are questions as to why a new, larger church was needed; many theories are connected to the Templars. In any case, the new church was never completed, hence its name, *L'Incompiuta*. The shell is a mystical-looking apparition, with lots of intriguing symbols that keep those theories circulating. The complex was under the Benedictines, and work went slowly, some say for lack of money, but when the Benedictine order was suppressed by Pope Bonifacio VIII in 1297, the complex was given to (can you guess?) the Cavalieri dell'Ordine dell'Ospedale di San Giovanni di Gerusalemme –aka the Templar Knights. The knights decided, however, to make their headquarters in the Palazzo del Balì in town (now a hotel) and the whole thing was scrapped.

The theories speculate that the true intention of the new church was to house something precious that was then taken elsewhere, making the whole project useless. For one, Robert Guiscardo played a role in the Venosa church (he is buried in the Chiesa Antica, along with his brothers, first wife and son), and he also ordered the construction of the cathedral in Acerenza (#51). With the lore surrounding *that* cathedral, the theories are interesting.

The Incompiuta builders handily used stone blocks from the adjacent Roman site, so you'll see Latin inscriptions and Roman carvings embedded in the walls. There are also some Hebrew inscriptions. Over the entry door, the lunette with a lamb and a cross was a Templar symbol. This whole place is crawling with fascinating engravings and emblems, so keep your eyes open!

The Chiesa Antica is also intriguing. The front façade shows the various add-ons to the structure. The main entry door is the one flanked by two stone lions. To the right, the arcades and blocky structure were added as the monastic residence. Looking to the left of the door are staggered additions from the Norman period, with the furthest left the oldest section of the church. Inside, are tombs of the ruling families, most notably Roberto Guiscardo, here labeled the Terror Mundi (terror of the world, don't think I would have wanted to meet this guy). My favorite thing in this church is the Column of Friendship, a Roman column placed here in the vestibule, on the left side by the door. They say that joining hands round it will seal your friendship for eternity. Obviously, it is a popular place for wedding couples to come for photos.

Also in the left nave, you'll see pavement from the original basilica; down on the lower level, mosaics from the Roman age, disputed whether from a home or the old pagan temple.

But I promised you three abbeys. Back outside, next to the Incompiuta you'll see a shamrock-shaped ruin. It was part of the early 5th century church, and they say within that lovely part was the baptismal font. You'll see more of the church's outline in the ruins. Access to the Incompiuta is through the archeology site and well worth the meager entrance fee.

While you're here, go across the street from the complex to see where the Roman amphitheater was located.

When you cross the street from these old abbeys, a recreation of the Beatles' infamous Abbey Road photo is in order, don't you think?

See: https://www.comune.venosa.pz.it/turismo (Italian only)

47. Enjoy a Pedal-Powered Day at a Volcanic Lake

Looming over Rionero in Vulture is the namesake mountain, Monte Vulture (pronounced VOOL-too-ray) that is actually an extinct volcano. It last erupted some 40,000 years ago, but it left behind two legacies: the naturally-effervescent mineral-rich water that is bottled here and shipped all over Italy (and beyond); and a graceful pair of small lakes, the Laghi di Monticchio, that are immersed in the crater, surrounded by thick forest.

You can walk around the entire area, of course, but why not have more fun and pump your legs on the pedal boats that take you away from the shore? Glide alongside the ducks to get a picturesque vantage point of the gleaming white monastery on the hill above, sitting pretty amongst the verdant trees. Bring a picnic to enjoy right on your boat as you enjoy the cooling water of Lago Piccolo.

If you prefer to stay on land, don't think you can just sit around. Okay, you can. But then you'd miss out on the four-person bicycle-like contraption that lets you circle the lake under the umbrella of cooling trees. Park it and walk up to the monastery (more on that below; someone should stay with the cart, though). Stop to enjoy a sip of something cool or a gelato along the way, as there are kiosks scattered about. The *bici* are especially fun if you have three or four people to pedal and laugh with. (Tip: If you want to slouch off, get in the back. They won't know you're not pedaling. Not that I would ever.) The paved path makes it easy going.

However you do it, your legs will get a work-out. You cannot leave the lakes without walking up to the Abbazia di San Michele Arcangelo. The historic site was founded in the 8th century as a simple hermitage in a grotto. Over the years it expanded, but the grotto with 9th century frescoes is still there and active, and a spiritual place of prayer. The abbey offers stunning views over the butterfly-shaped lakes, and a natural history museum occupies the lower floors if you want to expand your knowledge about the flora and fauna of the area.

The Laghi di Monticchio is usually a quiet spot and generally uncrowded, unless you come in August, or in autumn, when half of Puglia shows up to forage for mushrooms and chestnuts in these woods. There are food stands and restaurants for refreshment. They won't offer you a stellar dining experience, but will fill your hunger. I recommend bringing along a picnic, though, to make the most of the day. Restaurants in Rionero in Vulture are a higher caliber, if it's a "real meal" you're after.

There is no entrance or parking fee to experience the Laghi di Monticchio, but of course you'll pay rental charges for the boats and bikes.

48. FOLLOW THE FOOTSTEPS OF HISTORY IN MELFI

When people talk about Basilicata as "historically impoverished and remote" I point them to Melfi. The city sits below the brooding Mt. Vulture, where rolling hills give way to wavy wheat fields. An ancient Lucania city called Melpes, it was cited by Pliny in his volume on Roman history, and ran the usual course from Lucani to Greek to Roman inhabitants, but it was the Norman rulers who brought destiny to Melfi and made it a city of great standing and a crossroads of culture.

Melfi was the capital of the Duchy of Puglia and Calabria in 1059 and was assigned by Pope Niccolo II to Robert Guiscardo, of Venosa fame (#46). It became, almost inexplicably, one of the most important towns in the Norman realm. Princes, popes and nobles met here, and history has been written here (literally). Pope Urban II launched the first Crusade to the Holy Land from here, and Frederick II gave the world its first set of written laws in the modern era.

It was Frederick II who rebuilt the town's landmark castle (#49) that became one of his court centers and summer residence. The **Norman walls** that still surround Melfi's old town are 4-kilometers long, the only standing Norman walls in southern Italy. Of the six city gates that permitted entrance through the walls, the most intriguing is the **Porta Venosina**, the one through which the emperor himself entered. (Only three gates remain today.)

The town retains its medieval urban layout with many surprises and delights hidden among the streets; the joy is walking around and finding them. The streets are lined with pastel and stone buildings hung with ornate iron balconies, some winding narrow lanes and lots of pretty corners. Go ahead and get lost in the maze (you can't stay lost for too long!)

Find the three ancient stone gates; walk into the depths of the courtyard at **Palazzo Aquilecchia**. Stop in the **cathedral**, originally built starting in 1076 on the orders of Robert Guiscardo. It has been rebuilt a few times; while it's been stripped of its original architectural styles, it is still worth a visit. But the really interesting thing is the free-standing **campanile** bell tower, which *did* survive from the Norman period. Notice the details and mosaics inlaid on its stones. Melfi is a friendly town, and there are plenty of restaurants to get off your feet and enjoy a sampling of Lucanian fare.

Obviously, the main sight here is the landmark castle and museum (#49). Let me just say, it's worth the trip to Melfi to see it.

Remember I said there are surprises here? Go to the **Carbone winery's** *bottaia* in the old town center to see what I mean. Besides a wine tasting, you'll get a trip down into the volcanic rock. (No more spoilers than that; just go!) While enjoying a local vintage think about how this seemingly out-of-the-way-place was touched by destiny and history.

49. Storm the Castle in Melfi

You can't miss it. Seriously. With 10 towers and surrounding walls, it is, in a word, impressive. The castle is the crowning feature of Melfi, and an intriguing one, at that. The dominating defensive structure was built at a strategic point between Campania and Puglia, and was never captured or subdued. That doesn't mean you can't storm across the moat and enter its stately realm.

As I mentioned in the previous entry, it was the Normans who came and put Melfi on the map and first turned this castle into the capital of their southern realm. Between 1059 and 1137, five ecumenical councils were held here by various popes, and it was here that Pope Niccoli II appointed Robert Guiscard as duke of Puglia and Calabria. Pope Urban II launched the first Crusade to the holy land from here.

In the Sveva period, Frederick II expanded the castle and gave it great importance in his empire. He gave the world its first set of written laws in the modern era; the Costituzioni Augustales (also known as the Constitutions of Melfi) were codified and applied to the Holy Roman Empire and Kingdom of Sicily in 1231. They are still called a "masterpiece of jurisprudence".

The castle was enlarged significantly in the Angevin period and modified again under the Aragons, when it became a regal residence for the feudal lords that included the Caracciolo family and then the Doria dynasty, whose property it remained right up until 1950.

In short, this one building has seen a lot of history. Luckily, the walls reverberate all those epochs, so go inside and hear the voices of the ages speak through the astounding array of exhibits in the Museo Archeologico Nazionale Melfese.

It is jam-packed with artifacts that include Frederick II coins, astounding ceramics, gold-leaf tiaras, impressively-detailed bronze sculptures, intricate carvings, ancient metal helmets and armor, and more. A highlight is the Sarcophagus of Rapolla, an adorned stone tomb that is a work of art. It is so pristine and its deep relief carvings of deities and heroes are so intact you'll think it was created a couple hundred years ago instead of a couple millennia, yet it was done in the 2nd century BC. On the lid, the superbly sculpted deceased lies in a peaceful sleep. The museum beautifully displays pieces from the Lucani, the Greeks, Romans, Byzantines, Normans and more. It really is a trip through time.

Outside, you can see how the Norman walls still surround the *centro storico*, and how this massive *castello* watched over the realm. Walk (or drive) around behind it for a truly impressive view. After the castle, walk along Via Santa Caterina to the park, Bosco Littorio. The green space is a great picnic spot.

With such a testimony to history, you'll be glad you came and invaded Melfi and its castle.

More information: https://www.basilicataturistica.it/en/turismi/the-norman-castle-of-melfi (English)

50. Sip One of Italy's Oldest Wines in the Shadow of a Volcano

It's no surprise that Roman-era writer Orazio (Horace) sang its praises; being from Venosa he heralded his birth land often, but other ancients also appreciated the rich, complex wine known as Aglianico del Vulture. Horace said that his preferred *vino* "imparts comfort, joy, and confidence". When Roman naturalist author Pliny wrote his Natural History, *Aglianico* was already so ingrained in the soil and on the tables that he called it an indigenous grape varietal. More recently, it has been dubbed, "the Barolo of the south," a moniker they take a bit of umbrage with here, countering that "Barolo is the Aglianico of the north!" They're not wrong; long before Barolo was born, *Aglianco* was being cultivated to excellence –six millennia before, in fact!

This wine grape is considered one of the oldest in Italy, brought to the south by Greek colonists in the 7th century BC. The name probably derives from those settlers who were smart enough to bring seeds and plant vineyards – Ellenico, or "of the Greeks". Another theory says the name comes more specifically from the Magna Grecia city of Elea (Velia), south of Salerno- *gli eleani*, those from Elea.

However it came, there is no doubt it has been here a very long time and that *Aglianico* has done well in the mineral-infused volcanic soil below Monte Vulture (#47). In fact, it is often listed as one of the "world's best wines". It can be a finicky grape to cultivate but is also very workable to achieve a vast range of wines, from light-bodied and fruity to deep, complex and full-bodied. That's great for imbibers, as it is never a boring bottle to open.

So, what are you waiting for? Visit a few vineyards to sample the excellence of this ancient grape. It is said to bring joy and comfort, after all, and who doesn't want a cup of that?

There are many, many wineries in the Vulture zone, producing excellent and award-winning wines; I can't list them all, so I'm giving you my personal favorites. Call or email to reserve a winery visit and tasting.

Venosa

Re Manfredi's gorgeous setting makes you want to sit down, open a bottle and just stay there enjoying the view and the *vino*. There's nothing stopping you, so go ahead. The 271-acre estate is positively idyllic, and enjoys a lovely panorama of Venosa. Luisa grew up in the U.S. and speaks excellent English.

Barile

Elena Fucci is a rockstar of aglianico, who took over her grandfather's vineyard twenty years ago and made it a commercial success. She still uses his original vines –some more than 70 years old- along with newer plants. She makes one single label, called Titolo, and it is sheer perfection. She is an impressario of simplicity, bringing out what best represents the heritage grape from the terroir, the climate and the tenacity of the Lucani spirit. Her cantina is a lovely one.

If Elena is a rock star, **Paternoster** is the *prima donna*, one of the first to start selling bottles of *Aglianico*, which previously had been produced primarily for family use. That was back in 1925, and they've racked up many awards since then and are generally hailed as the grand-daddy of *Aglianico del Vulture*. The sleek, modern winery is easy to find right off the SS 93 highway.

Rionero in Vulture

The **Cantina del Notaio** gets the award for most beautiful and interesting winery. The cantina, on the main street of Rionero in Vulture, is actually below the streets of the city. Book a tasting tour and descend into the stone-lined underground rooms to see the traditional aging casks and a charming hand-made Christmas village as a bonus. Upstairs, the tasting room is modern; they are noted for excellence in each label. They also produce one of the region's best *rosato* wines, for rosé fans.

What **Strappellum** lacks in beauty at its winery, it makes up for in the bottle. I'm highlighting this one because in a region where the attention all goes to the reds, this winery takes that *Aglianico* grape and produces exceptional whites from it. The Nibbio Bianco is golden, highly aromatic and full-bodied; also try the Millesimato sparkling white and the sparkling red, as little attention goes to those either. Of course, they have some fine reds, as well.

51. Search for the Holy Grail and Other Mysteries in Acerenza

There is a lot of legend, mystery and drama regarding the Templars and it can be hard to tell fact from fiction – or just good storytelling. What we do know is that an order of the Knights Templar was born in Basilicata; and that the first crusade was planned and launched here (#49). Forenza, Venosa, Castelmezzano and Acerenza all certainly had strong Templar ties.

Then things get murky, mystic, and a little weird. The stories involve Pythagoras, French connections, Leonardo da Vinci, and of course, the holy grail. If Dan Brown's books aren't enough and you want to track down traces of the Knights Templar for yourself, then Acerenza is the place for you.

The Holy Grail trail goes back to when the region was still called Lucania, when the Normans arrived. But even before *that*, there was a certain monk named Canio (or Canius, and also Canione). Now, bear with me. This obscure saint is venerated in only two towns in Italy – Acerenza and Calitri. His remains were brought to Acerenza by Bishop Leone II in 799. Little is known about him, but his name is said to mean "superb watcher." In any case, Canio's bones were sealed in a crypt in a church in Acerenza, the earlier cathedral from the 6th or 7th century, when Acerenza became a diocese. That church had been built over a Roman temple dedicated to Hercules, which was standing when Pythagoras was in Metaponto (#7). Keep this in mind.

When the Norman warrior Robert Guiscardo took Acerenza in 1061, he set about building a new cathedral and installed as archbishop a certain Arnoldo, a church-building mystic from Cluny, France who constructed this particular cathedral using "the secret knowledge" and "sacred measurements." When it was completed in 1080, it revealed some very strange symbols and intriguing mysteries that are still being pondered.

This church, they say, was built by members of a secret Templar society using the Biblical proportions of "20 cubits by 60 cubits" as directed for the *sancta sanctorum* in Solomon's Temple in Jerusalem. The overall scheme is of absolute geometry, the so-called "golden section" referred to by Dan Brown, and the sacred geometry of Pythagoras. They say. Why was it used for this cathedral? And why was such a grand cathedral built for such a small community? What is certain is this is no ordinary church, and it was built in this highly defensive aerie to house something of value.

Let's look at a few other mysteries and symbols here. The footprint of this church is nearly identical to the uncompleted church in Venosa (#46), also of Norman and Guiscard fame, leading to theories that Acerenza was chosen and the Incompiuta of Venosa's primary purpose became irrelevant, thus never completed. The Prior of Venosa, Berengario, was also from Cluny. Pope Urban II, who planned and launched the first crusade from nearby Melfi, was Abbot of Cluny before coming here. (Forget Rennes le Chateau, Cluny is the key.)

There are gargoyles guarding the entrance, along with many Templar symbols and Maltese crosses on the façade, and oddly pagan ones, too. There is an absence of traditional Christian crosses inside, and the strange presence of a bust of Flavio Claudio Giuliano, called Giuliano the Apostate, an emperor who persecuted Christians.

In the sanctuary, one window is placed higher than the others. This opening and its opposing window join their rays of sunlight on one day a year, converging together on May 25, St. Canio's feast day. Whoever designed it had a profound knowledge of astronomy and optics, as well as geometry.

In the crypt is a black window where metal detectors reportedly go berserk. And then there is the mystery of St. Canio's magic staff, resting on an ancient stone altar in a sealed chamber. It can be seen through a circular opening and is said to move spontaneously, sometimes close enough to the opening to touch it, other times farther away. And, it sometimes levitates. (Cue Twilight Zone music.) What's in that closed-up chamber? Is the altar hiding something else?

Leonardo da Vinci figures in, too. He was friends with the Segni family who had a *palazzo* in Acerenza, and, it is theorized, may have visited while searching for traces of Pythagorean knowledge, which, during the Renaissance, was apparently a thing with intellectuals. He gifted a self-portrait of himself to Antonio Segni, and it was found here in Acerenza in 2008, after centuries of obscurity; it had for years assumed to be a painting of Galileo. It was authenticated by the Museum of Leonardo in his hometown of Vinci and by the Biblioteca Reale di Torino. Intriguing, no?

And who was St. Canio anyway? Who was this "superb watcher" and what was he guarding? Was he really a bishop from Carthage? Maybe he isn't who they thought at all. A few think he may have been a knight from Gaul, or a Templar who returned from the Holy Sepulcre. Or maybe…

Pythagorean knowledge was transmitted by the master to his students, who carried it on through a sort of confraternity or secret sect. Perhaps that "sacred knowledge" became a treasure entrusted to the Templar Knights? Maybe it is Pythagoras himself who is buried here in a temple built using his wisdom? The secrets held here may be the Pythagorean legacy sealed away, he that "great watcher" of the universe. Or maybe it really is the holy grail or another sacred relic enclosed within the enigma and mystery of Acerenza's cathedral. Look at the signs and symbols for yourself. You may just reveal an unsolved mystery with your search.

More information on the Templars in Basilicata:
https://www.basilicataturistica.it/sulle-orme-dei-templari
(Italian only).

52. Travel the World in One Region
– or Pretend To

Whether you're an unrepentant Instagrammer or not, photo ops have been a part of travel since "Kodak moments." Admit it, you've posed and preened at a location to get the right shot and share it with your friends. With social media, travel photos go to a whole different level.

Regardless of your pic-snapping penchants, you may just have a sense of humor and want to fake out your friends to keep them guessing where you are. Here in Basilicata you can make them think you're traveling all over the world –by snapping pictures in some opportune places.

The Basilicata tourism bureau even ran a commercial about the region's resemblances to world destinations by displaying photos with the questions: Scotland? Egypt? Brazil? and then debunking it with the response, "No, Basilicata".

If you want to have a little fun with your Instagram account and leave your friends in confusion, then here are some places around the region that will let you photo-psych them.

Scotland. Visit one of Basilicata's castles and let your friends think you're storming around the Scottish Highlands. Good stand-ins are Melfi Castle (especially when photographed from the back side), Brienza, Brindisi di Montagna, or Moliterno. (All are in the Potenza province.)

Egypt or Tunisia. Pretend you're on an Egyptian desert or beach by visiting the soft sandy expanses of the Ionian shore. **Marina di Pisticci** is a good spot, whether you snag just the unpopulated length of sand or snap it with the water, too, both can stand in easily for Egypt or Tunisia.

Greece. It takes no stretch of the imagination to believe you're in Greece when you're at the temple of Hera in **Metaponto**. Called Le Tavole Palatine, the Greek colony here built them just like "back home".

Rio de Janeiro. With the hulking statue of Christ standing tall over the steep hill and the sea below, it's a no-brainer that **Maratea** is the perfect pose-spot to pretend you're in Rio. Just don't expect to party like you're in Rio, as this is just a tad sleepier.

Jerusalem. Since **Matera** has been the movie double for many Biblical films, it's the obvious choice. Anywhere in the Sassi Caveoso will do nicely.

Arizona. Surprise, Basilicata has its own canyon lands that offer lovely drives. While you're not going to fool anyone into thinking you're at the Grand Canyon (there is only one of those!) you can certainly make them guess that you're in the Southwest with some of the scenery you'll find around **Aliano, or Noepoli,** along the **SS 653 Sinnica Road,** or the **Val d'Agri SS 598 road** around **San Martino d'Agri, Gallicchio, Missianello** zone.

Turkey. The captivating abbey in **Venosa** can stand in for several places in Turkey depending on the angle you choose, so take your pick. Want to be in Antioch? Or Didyma, maybe? Perhaps Perga-Aksu is to your taste. Or maybe you'd prefer to make them guess you're in Amman Jordan; from certain corners of the Chiesa Incompiuta, that's doable, too.

Smile, and say cheese!

BASILICATA'S FOODIE DELIGHTS

One of the great things about Italian cuisine is that it's never boring. Each region, even small swaths within regions, have their distinct dishes and food specialties, so traveling around gives us new things to sample.

Basilicata has its own ingrained culinary delights, many stemming from the region's humble roots, the *"cucina povera"* that led to creativity in the kitchen using simple ingredients to create delectable dishes. The products from here are *genuino*, for the most part made like they've been for centuries. It's a great region for vegetarians, because many dishes utilize legumes and the season's veggies, but carnivores won't go hungry, either. Here are some of the things to savor while you're in Basilicata.

Caciocavallo Podolico. A cow's milk cheese made from the mountain-grazing *podolico* breed of cattle, *caciocavallo podolico* from Basilicata is one of Italy's most prized (and priciest!) cheeses. This cheese isn't used in cooking but is savored. It's especially delicious when drizzled with local chestnut honey. (#40)

Cavatelli pasta. The pasta here is made without eggs (great for vegans!), and the preferred shape is *cavatelli*. Hand-shaped by dragging little pasta nubs across the pastry board with three fingers, it retains little pockets that hold the savory sauces. Whether it's an everyday tomato *ragú*, a vegetable sauce with chickpeas, or with cooked *rapini* greens, the shape holds up well to the vast variety of toppings. *Orecchiette* (little ears) and wider, flatter *strascinati* (literally, "dragged") are also popular pasta shapes you'll find here.

Peperoni Cruschi. Long, thin sweet peppers that are dried in the sun then fried in olive oil, they're eaten whole or crumbled on top of *cavatelli* pasta. They're found only in Basilicata. They are often combined with *mollica di pane* (course bread crumbs) that are seasoned and fried in olive oil, the combination sprinkled over pasta, a poor-man's cheese substitute. I warn you, *peperoni cruschi* are easily addictive. (#23)

Lucanica sausage. Real *lucanica* is made from selected pieces of pork and fat, both of which are cut by hand into small cubes (not ground), spiced with salt, pepper, ground *peperone dolce* (from those peperoni cruschi) and wild fennel seeds. The spicy version adds *piccante* chile powder to the mix. Either way, it's moist and delicious, and is used in pasta sauce, simmered in wine, or grilled. (#31)

Related to Lucanica, sort of, is *pezzente*, a more-humble sausage that is fattier and uses some of the less-prized parts of the pig, and is often used in sauce or aged to make salami.

Carne di cavallo. Horse meat is a thing in southern Italy and in Emilia-Romagna, but in towns around Matera, like Bernalda, and just across the border in Puglia, it is a passion, especially when enjoyed in a *braceria*. Specialized butchers raise and sell the meat in their shops, which turn into wood-fired grill-restaurants in the evening. You select the meat you want and they cook it to perfection while you wait. Some offer a smattering of side dishes, along with local red wine to accompany the grilled meat.

Acquasale. An ingenious dish, it means "salt water" but is a way of using stale bread, with as many recipes as there are cooks. Generally, a light broth is made of onions or other vegetables, along with *peperoni cruschi* or tomatoes and water. Eggs are poached in the broth and it's all spooned over the bread in bowls.

Cialledda. Found more often around Matera, it is a dish of dry bread that is rehydrated, onions, cucumbers, tomatoes and olives, drizzled with quality olive oil, sort of like the Lucania version of Tuscany's *panzanella*.

Lamb. We see lots of sheep around Basilicata, so you can bet the lamb dishes are truly tasty. Whether it's simply grilled or baked with wine and herbs, or topped with *mollica di pane*, we enjoy its sweet-and-savory flavor immensely. Mutton is used to make a stew called *cutturiedde*.

Likewise, those grazing sheep provide milk that is used to make swoon-worthy **Pecorino cheese**. We buy from a local producer in our village, but the varieties made in Filiano and Moliterno (called Canestrato) are both aged in grottoes, and are especially noteworthy and prized in other parts of Italy, as well.

Ricotta. The fresh ricotta of Basilicata is swoon-worthy; it's so creamy and light I say it's like eating a cloud. It can be made with cow's milk or sheep's milk. *Ricotta dura*, also called *ricotta salata* is set aside to dry and age a couple of weeks. Then it's grated over pasta, and hoo-boy, the way it melts on…*buonissimo*.

Rafanata. An unusual dish found only in this part of Italy, it uses *ráfano* (horseradish) which is referred to as "poor man's truffle". *Rafanata* is basically a frittata of eggs, potatoes or stale bread, grated horseradish and pecorino cheese, though some cooks add crumbled sausage or various herbs. It's usually served around Carnevale time for a spicy, warming kick during the festivities.

Bread. Forget that saltless, mealy bread of central Italy, here we enjoy heavenly loaves with crunchy crusts and soft interiors. It's made from *semola* flour (the stuff used for pasta) and often baked in wood-fired ovens. The contorted-shaped Matera bread has special protected (IGP) status and Slow Food recognition, and is considered by many to be the best bread in Italy. (#5)

Ciambotta. A popular local dish, it's made with potatoes, peppers, eggplant and tomatoes, all grown under the strong southern sun and picked fresh, mixed up together in a sort of ratatouille. Some cooks add an egg or two; others put in zucchini. It depends on what you have on hand. The word is also used a verb in these parts, *ciambottare*, meaning to throw something together, or to wing it.

Crapiata. A Materana dish, it is a filling vegetarian delight of grains and beans, slow-cooked, preferably in a clay pot in the fireplace. I'm not going to speculate on the origins of the name. ;)

Desserts. Honestly, they're not much to get excited about unless you encounter the *crustole*, a thin rosette of dough that is fried and drizzled with local honey. The *taralli glassati* of Avigliano are big lumpy donut-shaped dry cakes glazed with sugar topping. *Ravioli dolci*, also called *cauzencidd'or calzoncini* are made around *carnevale* and Christmas-time, usually with chocolate-chestnut or chocolate-chickpea filling, and those are tasty. In Bernalda, the almond-based, chocolate-lathered cookie called *scorzette* should finish off any meal.

TEN STAND-OUT RESTAURANTS THAT WILL MAKE YOUR TRIP TASTY

1. San Fele – Café Blues Tipicamente. That name means "typically" but there isn't much that is typical about this stellar restaurant. For starters, it defies the mountain-dwellers' no-fuss attitude of the area; and then there is the totally imaginative use of the region's products that you've read about in this book, in atypical ways. The chef's offerings draw clients from around the region, from Naples, and Salerno. The menu changes seasonally, presented nicely but without so much fuss you feel like they spend more time playing with your food than cooking it. The skilled *pizzaiolo* on duty in the evenings turns out Neapolitan-crusted pies in (what else) non-traditional toppings. The dining room *is* typical – exposed stone walls and Old World charm.

2. Montescaglioso – La Locanda dell'Abate. A tiny *osteria* cloistered away in the glossy limestone lanes of pretty Montescaglioso, near the intriguing Abbazia di San Michele. The chef is especially skilled at seafood specialties, but also offers veg and meat menus, and highlights certain ingredients at times, like the area's black truffles. But the fish! He turns the fresh catch into works of art on each plate. He will ask about your likes, dislikes and allergies, then go to work and bring out attractive and scrumptious dishes to suit. Do NOT skip the antipasto! The full menu is still an affordable meal (meaning you won't be dinged with a $250 check for two by leaving it in his capable hands.) The place is tiny, so do reserve in advance.

3. Maratea – Zà Mariuccia. This place is rather renowned, having been in business since 1958. Nonna sits in the kitchen overseeing everything so you can expect a good meal. The dining room exudes quiet elegance with crystal wine glasses and soft music, but most people covet the balcony for its romantic view over the water. Its location at the port means that seafood is certainly fresh, but they don't overlook the area's other land-based recipes, either. In fact, Zà Mariuccia is a Buon Ricordo restaurant and their selected regional plate is ravioli with lamb sauce (swoon). Buon Ricordo is a program of "happy memories" and you get a hand-painted plate to take home as a keepsake when you order that dish.

4. Maschito – Masseria Sett'Anni. Reserve a meal at this farm restaurant out in the country beyond town and prepare yourself for a never-ending feast. Or at least it feels like it may never end, as plate after plate comes out: local cheese dribbled with honey, *ciambotta*, *rafanata*, grilled vegetables, and more. The *antipasto* alone bears eight or more heaping samplers that may make you want to say "*basta*," and stop there, but resist that notion because the pasta and mains are worth the belt-busting that may follow. Served with local Maschito wine, this full monty experience is one of a kind, and the type of feast worth indulging in that every trip needs. Everything is prepared with local seasonal ingredients and the offerings change regularly.

5. Castelmezzano – Il Becco della Civetta. With a panorama of the looming Dolomiti Lucane peaks, if you can get a table on the balcony, all the better. But no matter where you sit, the meal will be spectacular, as chef Maria Antonietta is a perfectionist. She takes Basilicata's traditional dishes and gives them a dose of "oomph". Whether it's the *strascinati con peperoni cruschi* or the filling *lagane e ceci* (pasta with chickpeas), or local ricotta stuffed inside ravioli, everything is delicious. Save room for house-made desserts! The menu changes regularly, and she will prepare excellent meals for celiac, vegetarians, vegans on request.

6. Venosa – L'Incanto Ristorante. Also called the Accademia dei Piacevoli, or "the academy of pleasures" -as in dining pleasure. And so, it's pretty much guaranteed you're going to be pleased with your meal when that's where they set the bar. They take exacting measures in everything, from the table settings to the ambiance to the plating, but all that would be for naught if the dishes weren't top-notch. They give creative twists to timeless classics and add a touch of whimsy to the area's locally-grown products, what the chef calls "an enogastronomic journey." It's an elegant, relaxing and...yes pleasurable, experience.

7. Matera – Ristorante Baccus. If I had to choose only one restaurant that represents Matera's atmosphere and fare, it would be Baccus. Indoors, the cave-like rooms hewn out of the tufa rock are totally "Sassi" style, but livened up by the pieces of festival lighting-turned-chandeliers. It is stylish yet homey at the same time. There is an outdoor patio too. They bring Matera's time-honored recipes to delicious heights, and serve it with a joke and a smile. Bar none, my Matera favorite. Ask to see the wine cellar.

8. Terranova del Pollino – Luna Rossa. Imagine a blending between down-home trattoria ambiance and Michelin-worthy cuisine. That's Luna Rossa, run by Federico Valicenti, Basilicata's first celebrity chef. The jovial *cuoco* is an excellent host who is also scrupulous to everything, which makes the out-of-the-way restaurant at the foot of the Pollino National Park a destination dining experience. Choose one of the tasting menus for the best full-on experience, but you can't go wrong no matter what you order. Chef Federico is legendary.

9. Lavello – Antica Cantina Forentum. Little out-of-the-way Lavello in the northern Vulture zone may not seem like a grand attraction, but this restaurant sure is. The young owners bring passion and pride in the region to their cozy restaurant with high level cuisine made from regional goods. A mix of surf and turf satisfies every palate, and everything is made in-house, including the bread. Perfect pizzas are also turned out of the wood-burning oven. Excellent all around. (They also have designer rooms if you're looking for a comfortable place to spend a night or two.)

10. Potenza – Ristorante le Antiche Torri. At the edge of Potenza's *centro storico* below the ancient towers, the classic atmosphere is punctuated with splashy modern art. That's sort of a precursor of the cuisine – old time nana's recipes with a burst of new life. Pasta is handmade, service is cordial and pizzas are Naples-good. It's worth the hassle of getting up to the *centro* to dine here. It's small so reserve a table. Open for dinner only. (Ride the escalator up #30.)

Hotels In Basilicata

There seems to be no "happy medium" in Basilicata – either you have too many choices, like in Matera, or you have few choices, and those can be hard to locate. To help you plan your trip, I'm listing a few of the accommodation options around the region. My taste may not be the same as yours, of course, and there are booking sites and options to explore online. The hotels and B&Bs listed here were valid at the time of publication.

MATERA. There are hundreds of lodgings in Matera; these are a few that I like, in various price points.

Residenza San Giorgio. This is my personal go-to place, located within a lovely *recinto*, each suite has a kitchenette and outdoor space. They were all restored by the owners themselves, who provide excellent service.

Palazzo Viceconte. A palace near the cathedral with a spectacular panoramic rooftop, palatial salons and spacious rooms.

At the bottom of the Sassi two properties stand out: **Le Dimore dell'Idris**, just below the rocky pinnacle church of Santa Maria dell'Idris with excavated cave rooms have splashy locally-crafted furnishings; and **Corte San Pietro** where the 13 rooms cluster around a courtyard, each one conforming to the cave structure and beautifully done.

On the level Civita at Piazza del Sedile, the **Residenza dei Suoni** is a lovely four-room B&B where you can hear the music from the piazza, in a convenient location.

Palazzo Del Duca is an upscale boutique hotel with excellent details, a spa (massage, anyone?) and some rooms with romantic, relaxing jet tubs.

Vicolo Fiore B&B is cozy, whimsical and welcoming, at a great price.

BERNALDA AND THE IONIAN COAST AREA

In Bernalda, the ritzy **Palazzo Margherita** gets the most attention (of course). If you want a splurge place, this is it. In the *centro storico* of Bernalda, the more affordable but well-appointed **Borgo San Gaetano** offers beautifully-renovated suites, helpful staff, and better prices.

Montescaglioso. Between Matera and Bernalda, the pretty town of Montescaglioso is listed among "the most beautiful village in Italy" and also has one of my featured dining experiences. Here, an *albergo diffuso* **Il Borgo Ritrovato** has nice suites placed in restored houses around the old town center.

Beach Hotel. **Masseria Macchia and Relais San Pio** is a pretty estate with working farm, well-furnished rooms, a pool, spa, and private beach at Marina di Pisticci.

Between *Pisticci* and Marina di Pisticci, the **Masseria Torre Fiore** is a swanky resort hotel in a lovingly restored farmhouse complex, with all the amenities you could want and an excellent restaurant.

Tursi. The **Orangery Retreat** with two apartments, gorgeous touches, cooking classes and quiet corners is a relaxing choice. **Colobraro's Antica Masseria Lucana** offers six mini-apartments, pool and terrace, horse stables and restaurant.

MARATEA. The city is spread out in many districts, and there are many choices. These are a few I like.

La Locanda delle Donne Monache. Up at the top of Maratea's old town, this beautifully-restored monastery has comfy beds, a garden and pool, and shuttle service to the beach.

Hotel Villa del Mare is a resort hotel with sea views, pool and spa, and private beach at Acquafredda.

Hotel Murmann is modern hotel just a few steps from Fiumicello Beach, with pool, A/C and breakfast buffet. If you want beachside, **Hotel Settebello** is rather basic but is right on the sand.

Hotel Borgo La Tana is a family-run hotel complex and what I call "American style" with spacious rooms, a gym, pool, big breakfast buffet, train station and beach shuttle, powerful A/C, and the bonus of an excellent restaurant on-site.

If it's luxury you want, then **Hotel Santa Venere** is the place. The five-star property has all the exclusivity and amenities you want, including spa, three restaurants, and VIP-style private beach.

Rotonda. A jumping-off point for the wilderness of the Pollino National Park, Rotonda's **Borgo Ospitale** has suites scattered in renovated homes around the old town, all very nicely furnished. If you'd rather be out in nature, the **Calivino Agriturismo** is a three-room farm stay with home-cooking restaurant.

Viggiano's **Dimora del Musicante B&B** has rooms in the former home of one of Viggiano's traveling musicians, in the old town. Outside the city the **Agriturismo Masseria San Michele** is a rural stone inn with home-cooked meals at a high elevation for starry nights.

Most of the hotels around *Grumentum* are pretty blah, but the **Agriturismo La Vecchia Quercia** has three comfortable rooms and fabulous farm-fresh meals.

Senise has two lake-front properties that let you relax and enjoy views of the water. The **Agriturismo Pagliarone** is the Donna Perna farm (*peperoni cruschi*!) while **Casata del Lago** is more resorty with a pool, lawns and restaurant.

DOLOMITI LUCANE

There are several B&Bs in **Castelmezzano** – try **the Casa del Mago** or **Casa dell'Arco**; for hotel service, the **Hotel Castromediano** is perfect for its views and hospitality. In **Pietrapertosa**, the *albergo diffuso* **Le Costellazioni or Palazzo del Barone** are good choices. Outside **Trivigno,** the *agriturismo* **La Foresteria di San Leo** is a secluded, gated estate with well-appointed rooms, two apartments, gorgeous views, pool, and restaurant just for guests. Between **Calvello and Abriola**, the farm-stay **BioAgriturismo Sant'Elia** has six rooms, a working organic farm, and home-produced meals, run by young dynamic owners.

VENOSA

The **Hotel Orazio** is set in the historic Palazzo del Bali' that once belonged to the Templars; modern rooms with A/C and elevator, helpful hosts, and an upscale restaurant.

The cozy **B&B Le Dimore degli Artisti** is boutique-style with very basic breakfast. Go all-out at the just-outside-town *agriturismo* **Tenuta Lagala** wine resort.

MELFI

In the old town, the **Casa del Borgo Antico** is a comfy, boutique-type B&B, as is the **Stanze dell'Imperatore**. If you want a modern hotel, look to **Relais La Fattoria**, a Holiday Inn-style hotel with pool, big rooms, and big beds.

Note: I do not receive commissions or perks for these referrals. They are meant as a helpful resource. Please let me know if something has changed or closed, or if you found something rave-worthy you want to share!

Resources

DRIVERS AND TOUR SERVICES

As I mentioned in the introduction, getting around the region is much easier with a rental car. But if you really don't want to drive, there are some other options.

PRIVATE DRIVERS

There are several licensed drivers who can take you where you want to go. (NCC means *noleggio con conducente*, or car hire with driver.) Here are a few I can recommend:

Potenza (and beyond) – Donato Palermo, Euroservice NCC; look for Euroservice NCC on Facebook. I've personally used Donato's services for family and clients, and he is professional, punctual and patient.

Matera – Services include transfers to/from Bari airport or trail station, around Matera and Basilicata, and Puglia.

NCC Matera; www.nccmatera.com
NCC Fabrizio; www.nccfabrizio.it

TOUR GUIDES AND TOUR COMPANIES

MATERA: There are many licensed guides to give you excellent indepth tours of Matera. I can highly recommend Amy Weideman, an American who has lived in the city for two decades. Find her at www.materatours.net

Matera Turismo (www.materaturismo.it), Discovery Matera (www.discoverymatera.it) and Matera City Tour (www.materacitytour.it) are a few others.

The adorable Ape tours are a fun way to get an overview. www.apeneisassi.it; www.apevito.com; and www.apecalessinotourmatera.com all offer the cute rides.

POLLINO: Find hiking, tubing, acqua-trekking and other excursions through Info Pollino (www.infopollino.com).

If you're looking for a guide to take you to the peaks and hidden mountain glories on foot, contact Giuseppe Cosenza, contatti@viaggiarenelpollino.it. (www.viaggiarenelpollino.it)

MELFI, VENOSA AND MORE: The expert guides at **Minutiello Travel** can take you to all the noted sights and locales around the region, including Melfi, Venosa, Craco, Castelmezzano and more. (www.minutielloviaggi.com)

Outdoors Adventures Pescopagano/San Fele zone: Enjoy trekking, climbing, acqua-trekking, and more through **Basilicata Sport & Adventure**. (www.basilicatasportadventure.com)

For something different, the **Jonian Dolphin Conservation** offers dolphin sighting trips from Taranto (Puglia) that cruise the Ionian coast of Basilicata. Skipper **Enrico Massocchi** organizes dolphin-watching outings from Policoro's Marinagri and Pisticci's Marina Argonauti, while **Circolo Velico Lucano** runs sailboat trips from Policoro for half-day, full-day or sunset cruises.

Horse riding, picnics, cycling, and special events tours in central Basilicata are organized by **Ivy Tour**.

Note: I do not receive any commission or perks for these referrals.

BUS COMPANIES AND RAIL LINKS TO BASILICATA
Trenitalia, the national rail service, called Ferrovia dello Stato: www.trenitalia.it

Italo Treno, a private high-speed rail company with train-bus links: www.italotreno.it

Autolinee Liscio – Bus service from Rome's Tiburtina station to Potenza and Matera: https://www.autolineeliscio.it

Marozzi Bus – Motor coach service from several central and northern cities to Potenza: www.marozzivt.it

FlixBus – an extensive network of buses around Italy, with many connections around the south, including Potenza and Matera: www.flixbus.it

Afterword

Thank you, *grazie*, dear reader for buying this book. My sincere wish is that you find it both enjoyable and helpful. Basilicata is a special place, and my desire is to help make it more easily approachable, and for travelers to step out of the "usual," and discover the many, many hidden gems that Basilicata has to offer.

Even after 10 years of living here, and despite its relatively small size, there are still places and events we've not yet experienced. Every town, every turn, reveals something interesting or beautiful, so I know your trip to Basilicata will not be boring. Be in touch; let me know about your discoveries along the way!

I've used my own first-hand knowledge, tourism experts, the region's tourism agency, and towns' Pro Loco community organizations for primary source information. I have made every attempt at accuracy but things can change, so do check online or through your lodgings' hosts before setting out, to make sure. If you note changes, do let me know.

There are loads of fun and interesting events; some of the dates change annually, though. Find a list on the Basilicata tourism website: www.basilicataturistica.it

Grazie...

Special thanks to my Nana Rose, who instilled her "Italianness" in me, and whose family came from the mountains of Basilicata. My own journey of genealogical discovery turned into a love for this land. Thanks to my *amore* Bryan for feeling the pull of this place and wanting to live here (and for everything you do, and all we share). To my *famiglia*, I thank you; love you to the moon. *Grazie* to Michelle Kaminsky for spearheading the concept and letting me run with it *-sei fantastica*. Thank you to my advance readers for the valuable input and proofreading help. A heartfelt and hearty thanks to Lisa Hamoy for creating the maps *-sei brava*! *Grazie tanto* to Marcella di Feo at APT Basilicata for giving assistance, encouragement, archive photos, and *pazienza*.

A very special *ringraziamento* to the Lucani, my *paesani*, who helped me assimilate and discover the many joys and gems of this unique region.

Wishing you all a *buon viaggio nella Lucania*. May you experience the kind of sacred hospitality and beauty the region is known for.

Tante belle cose,

Valerie
valerie.trivigno@gmail.com

PHOTO CREDITS

A special and heartfelt thanks to those who graciously provided photos when my own were lacking or not of high enough quality. They help enrich the book, and I thank each of you. Grazie di cuore.

Introduction food photo: Kars Alfrink, CC BY 2.0 Flickr
Matera photo: Michele Buono, Matera videographer and photographer
Chapter 1: provided by Locanda di San Martino Matera
Chapter 2: Piazza Sedile from Cinzia Astorino CC-SA 4.0
Chapter 9: Sea turtle from Stefano Bellomo, www.adventure-biologist.com
Chapter 19: Kayaks from Fly Maratea
Chapter 20: Pino Loricato Pollino by Francesco Cirigliano CC-BY 2.0 Flickr
Chapter 22: Riti Arborei from Ivy Tour, www.ivytour.it
Chapter 25: The Madonna Nera from Comune di Viggiano
Chapter 27: Fagioli from Sagra del Fagioli Sarconi
Chapter 28: Giacomo Silvano, CC BY-SA 4.0 via Wikimedia Commons
Chapter 31: Lucanica by Salumificio Carbone
Chapter 33: By craftsman Vito Summa, Balestra AViglianese
Chapter 34: Baccala dish from Osteria Gagliardi
Chapter 35: La Storia Bandita from Archivio APT Basilicata
Chapter 40: Caciocavallo by Caseificio Pessolani
Chapters 42, 44, and 51 Photos by friend and giornalista Raffaele Cutolo
Chapter 49: Memorato CC BY-SA 2.0

About The Author

Valerie Fortney is a freelance writer and professional genealogist who puts her B.A. in History to work by tracking down details of family histories and travel-related sights. She first traveled to Basilicata in 2003 with her mother and sister; that first foray led to another trip with cousins and a then-85-year old great-aunt to better explore her ancestral towns. Not only did she discover relatives living in Basilicata, she found the region had wrapped itself around her heart. Valerie and her husband Bryan moved to the village of Trivigno in 2010, and have been there ever since.

She immerses in local life by participating in the grape harvest, town *festas,* and hanging out with her *paesani* in the piazza. Valerie writes for International Living, tourism-related websites, and travel publications. She loves a good cappuccino, talking to people, exploring historic places, and wandering any hill town she comes upon. She loves the mountains and the sea in equal measures.

Valerie and Bryan are also professional genealogists and help other descendants discover their roots in Basilicata. See www.mybellabasilicata.com for more information.

Follow me on Instagram: Valerie in Italy

Printed in Great Britain
by Amazon